der stress

University of Plymouth Library

Subject to status this item may be renewed
via your Voyager account

http://voyager.plymouth.ac.uk

Exeter tel: (01392) 475049
Exmouth tel: (01395) 255331
Plymouth tel: (01752) 232323

Young families under stress
Outcomes and costs of Home-Start support

Colette McAuley, Martin Knapp, Jennifer Beecham, Nyree McCurry and Michelle Sleed

JR
JOSEPH
ROWNTREE
FOUNDATION
1904
2004

The **Joseph Rowntree Foundation** has supported this project as part of its programme of research and innovative development projects, which it hopes will be of value to policy makers, practitioners and service users. The facts presented and views expressed in this report are, however, those of the authors and not necessarily those of the Foundation.

Joseph Rowntree Foundation
The Homestead
40 Water End
York YO30 6WP
Website: www. jrf.org.uk

Chapter 1 © Colette McAuley
Chapter 2 © Colette McAuley, Nyree McCurry, Michelle Sleed, Jennifer Beecham and Martin Knapp
Chapters 3, 4, 5 and 6 © Colette McAuley and Nyree McCurry
Chapters 7 and 8 © Martin Knapp, Jennifer Beecham and Michelle Sleed
Chapter 9 © Colette McAuley and Martin Knapp

First published 2004 by the Joseph Rowntree Foundation

A CIP catalogue record for this report is available from the British Library.

ISBN 1 85935 217 0   (paperback)
ISBN 1 85935 218 9   (pdf: available at www.jrf.org.uk)

Cover design by Adkins Design

Prepared and printed by:
York Publishing Services Ltd
64 Hallfield Road
Layerthorpe
York YO31 7ZQ
Tel: 01904 430033; Fax: 01904 430868; Website: www.yps-publishing.co.uk

Further copies of this report, or any other JRF publication, can be obtained either from the JRF website (www.jrf.org.uk/bookshop/) or from our distributor, York Publishing Services Ltd, at the above address.

Contents

List of figures

List of tables

Acknowledgements

Many people helped to make this research study possible. We would like to thank the Joseph Rowntree Foundation who provided the funding for the project and the JRF Advisory Group for their support and advice throughout the three and a half years of the study. We are grateful to Susan Taylor, Joseph Rowntree Foundation, who chaired the Advisory Group, and Dr Marjorie Smith, Thomas Coram Research Institute, Scientific Adviser to the Foundation. Thanks are also due to Professor Jane Aldgate, Open University; Professor Miranda Mugford, University of East Anglia; Mary Wilmont, Director of Social Services, Northern Health and Social Services Board; Sally Holterman, Independent Consultant; Valerie McGuffin and Kay Bews, Directors of Home-Start in Northern Ireland and England, respectively; Dr Ian Gibbs, University of York; and Naomi Eisenstadt, Chief Executive of Sure-Start.

Many people have assisted in the study and we want to acknowledge their excellent work. The child welfare statistical analysis was carried out by Dr Martin Dempster, Queen's University. We owe him particular thanks for his considerable contribution to the project. We are also grateful to Dr Eugene Mooney for providing statistical consultancy. Dr Donncha Hanna also provided assistance with the statistical analysis whilst Laura Duncan assisted with data inputting. Dr Katrina McLaughlin and Dr Laura Dunne provided research assistance in the last few weeks of the project. Administrative support was provided during the project by Michael Markwell, Julie Lee, Christina Cree, Angela Mehta, Glenys Harrison and Janice Dickson.

This study would not have been possible without the full co-operation of Home-Start. The research team particularly want to acknowledge the support of Brian Waller, Chief Executive, and Wendy Rose, Chairperson, and the Senior Management Team. We also want to thank Valerie McGuffin and Kay Bews, national directors in Northern Ireland and England, respectively, for their untiring commitment to the project. We were really fortunate in the level of co-operation of the Home-Start scheme organisers in both Northern Ireland and England. We are also indebted to the health visitors and their managers who referred all the Comparison families and some of the Study families.

Central to the success of the project, however, was the willingness of the parents to participate in the study. Having discussed their situations with the research team at the outset of the study, we were really pleased that so many parents were keen to share their progress with us at follow up. The research team are indebted to them and trust that they have inspired us to better understand and convey the position of young parents under stress.

Colette McAuley, School of Social Work, Queen's University, Belfast
Martin Knapp, Personal Social Services Research Unit, London School of Economics, London
Jennifer Beecham, Personal Social Services Research Unit, University of Kent, Canterbury
Nyree McCurry, School of Social Work, Queen's University, Belfast
Michelle Sleed, Personal Social Services Research Unit, University of Kent, Canterbury

April 2004

1 Background to the study and methodology

Legislative, policy and research background

The recent government green paper *Every Child Matters* (DfES, 2003) indicates the government's intention to place support for parents and carers at the centre of its approach to improving children's lives. This builds upon the stronger mandate given to family support in recent child-care legislation in England and Wales and Northern Ireland (NI) (The Children Act 1989; The Children (NI) Order 1995).

Since the time of the Audit Commission report (Audit Commission, 1994), it has been recognised that services such as family support should be offered where needs have been assessed and where there is a likelihood of beneficial outcomes for children and families. Hence it has become imperative for commissioners and service providers, many of whom are voluntary organisations, to produce evidence of effectiveness. These same groups are under increasing pressure to produce evidence of cost-effectiveness.

Within the UK conceptual debates about the study of effectiveness of social welfare interventions have tended to centre around the extent to which randomised controlled trials are appropriate and/or possible (Cullen and Hills, 1996; MacDonald, 1996; Oakley, 1996). The problems posed in evaluating community-based initiatives to support children and their families have been recognised (Lewis and Utting, 2001). The particular dilemma of maintaining scientific rigour while facing ethical and practical constraints has been addressed (Ghate, 2001). The development of the Social Care Institute of Excellence and the commissioning of a body of studies on the effectiveness and cost-effectiveness of services for children in need indicate the current government's concern with gathering such data to inform policy and funding decisions. A body of literature is also developing (Hill, 1999; McNeish *et al.*, 2002; McAuley *et al.*, 2004).

In any study of effectiveness, the first step is to define outcomes clearly. Outcome measurement, however, is a complex area. Outcomes for children and families need to be distinguished from service outputs such as the number of agency visits to a family. Outcomes can be measured at an individual, family, community or service system level (Pecora *et al.*, 1995; Parker, 1998). The need to have clear operationalised objectives and to differentiate between short-term, intermediate-term and long-term outcomes has also been emphasised (Knapp, 1984; Knapp and Lowin, 1998). Providing tangible outcome measures for family support initiatives has proved to be a considerable challenge (Tunstill and Aldgate, 2000).

Family support can take many forms, including support through volunteers from the community. Providing family support through the use of volunteers is in line with the Make A Difference government initiative (DH/SSI, 1996), encouraging volunteering and the strengthening of local communities. An example of such provision is Home-Start, which has been offering this service in the UK since 1973.

Home-Start offers volunteer support to families under stress where there is at least one child under 5 years of age. It predominantly offers this support through home visiting but group support may also be available in some areas. In June 2003 there were 330 schemes in England, Scotland, Wales and Northern Ireland (Home-Start, 2003). Schemes have been developed in rural and urban areas and support white and ethnic minority families. Internationally there are now more than 100 schemes. Each scheme is an independent charity with a multi-disciplinary management committee rooted in its own community. All schemes share the same constitution and standards and methods of practice. The latter sets out the broad aims of the organisation (Appendix 1).

Previous research on Home-Start has found high levels of reported parent satisfaction with the service, but more recent studies have emphasised the need for a study of the outcomes of Home-Start support for the families who receive it (Van der Eyken, 1982; Gibbons and Thorpe, 1989; Frost *et al.*, 1996, Rajan *et al.*, 1996; Shinman, 1994). However, to study the impact of the intervention on the well-being of children and families we need to be able to chart change on salient dimensions over time. Hence in 1997 the Northern Health and Social Services Board commissioned a preliminary study to develop/select appropriate outcome measures to facilitate an effectiveness study of Home-Start (McAuley, 1999).

The Family Support Outcomes Study (the preliminary study; McAuley, 1999) examined referral patterns, user issues and potential outcome measures for Home-Start support. The overall purpose of the study was to develop a rationale for the selection of outcome measures for a study of the effectiveness of Home-Start. Initially, information about the organisation was gathered from a review of the research literature, information from Home-Start policy documents and consultations with academics specialising in the field of child welfare outcome measurement. A 2-year survey of referrals to two Home-Start schemes was then undertaken. From this it was determined that the predominant referrers were health visitors and that there were five predominant reasons for referral:

- mother's mental health

- mother's physical health

- mother's isolation/loneliness

- multiple births/ multiple young children

- child/children with special needs.

Interviews were then carried out with 10 families who had just started to receive Home-Start support, 10 who had been in receipt of Home-Start support for 6 months and 10 who had just ceased to receive the support in the previous year. A focus group discussion was held, with parents attending a support group attached to one of the schemes. From the interviews and focus group discussion, three recurring themes emerged:

- parenting stress

- mother's self-esteem

- mother's social networks/perceived social support.

As a result five outcome domains were chosen: parental stress, maternal mental health, maternal social support, maternal self-esteem and child development. Psychometric tests relating to each of these domains were then reviewed regarding their appropriateness in measuring change in each of the specified domains. The final outcome measures agreed with Home-Start are outlined in Table 1. The results from this preliminary study (McAuley, 1999) laid the foundations for the current study.

The current study

Aim

The study had two aims, to evaluate the effectiveness of Home-Start support:

- in terms of outcomes and costs to children and their families experiencing specified stresses

- more specifically, in contributing to positive outcomes for children and parents where the family have been referred for selected reasons (maternal mental/physical health, social isolation, multiple births/young children and a child/children with special needs).

A third aim of the study had been to evaluate the effectiveness of Home-Start support with children and families of different ethnic origins,

Table 1 Selected outcome domains and measures

Outcome domain	Parenting stress	Maternal mental health	Maternal mental health	Maternal self-esteem	Child development	Maternal social support
Name of test	Parenting Stress Index (Abidin, 1995)	Edinburgh Postnatal Depression Scale (Cox et al., 1987)	Centre for Epidemiological Studies Depression Scale (Radloff, 1977)	Rosenberg Self-Esteem Scale (Rosenberg, 1965)	Brief Infant–Toddler Social and Emotional Assessment Scale (Briggs-Gowan and Carter, 2001)	Maternal Social Support Index (Pascoe et al., 1988)
Acronym	PSI/SF*	EPDS	CES-D	RSE	BITSEA	MSSI
Purpose	To assess sources and levels of stress in parents of children of up to 10 years of age	To screen for postnatal depression in the community	To measure the persistence and severity of depression	A measure of global self-esteem	To assess infant's social and emotional adjustment	Designed to assess the emotional and tangible support provided by a mother's social network
Reliability and validity	Extensive testing, robust diagnostic measure. Maintains validity across non-English-speaking cultures	Satisfactory validity and split half reliability, sensitivity to changes in the severity over time	High face validity, internal consistency, high test-retest reliabilities adequate. Established concurrent and construct validity with other indices of depression	Widely used although few psychometric data are available	Assessment of the validity and reliability of the scale ongoing	Acceptable internal consistency and concurrent and predictive validity. Test-retest validity across 9-month period reasonable
Description of scale	36-item derivative of 101-item test	10 items	20 items	10 items	60 items	18 items
Completion process	Self-report	Self-report	Self-report or administered	Self-report	Self-report	Self-report or part of interview
Estimated completion time	10 minutes	5 minutes	10 minutes	5 minutes	20 minutes	10 minutes

* PSI/SF: Parenting Stress Index Short Form Version

different sides of the divided community in Northern Ireland and from rural and urban communities. However, in the early stages of the study it became apparent that this aim would not be feasible for a number of reasons. Referrals to the study took much longer than anticipated and as a result we did not want to restrict the flow of referrals any further. We had hoped that the referrals would generate a sufficient diversity to be able to look at differences across families of different ethnic origin, but the referrals received related to mothers of almost entirely English/Northern Ireland white origin. With regard to examining divergence between different sides of the divided community, we were advised by senior health visitor managers that their staff would be unwilling to identify families as belonging to one community or another. They also indicated that, in their view, families would be deeply uncomfortable if asked about their perceived affiliation. Hence we decided not to include questions on this aspect. However, the research team was confident that the sample included families from different sides of the divided community in Northern Ireland and from rural and urban areas in both England and Northern Ireland.

Methodology

Ethical consent

The study was conducted in accordance with the Social Care Association Ethical Guidelines (Social Research Association, 2003). It was also approved by the three local research ethical committees covering the areas in Northern Ireland and England where the study was conducted.

Sample

In the study we had two groups of mothers with young children. The Study families were in receipt of Home-Start support while the Comparison families were not. The Study families were referred by Home-Start organisers or health visitors and the Comparison families were referred by health

visitors. The predominant reason for referral for all the families in the study fell within the five categories: maternal mental/physical health, social isolation, multiple births/young children and a child/children with special needs. The Study group families were drawn from 13 Home-Start schemes in Northern Ireland and eight schemes in south England. The Comparison families were drawn from a health and social services community trust in Northern Ireland and a health trust in southern England. Home-Start support was not available in the areas from which the Comparison families were drawn. The sample of 88 Study families and 89 Comparison families was achieved in May 2002. At the second-stage follow-up approximately 1 year later, a sample of 80 Study families and 82 Comparison families had been maintained. This meant that the retention rate was very high (91.5 per cent).

Interview format and content

First-stage interviews took place as soon as possible after the Home-Start service commenced with Study families and after referral with Comparison families. Second-stage interviews took place 10–12 months later. The mothers were interviewed in their own homes at a time convenient to them.

All of the mothers were initially interviewed through the use of a semi-structured interview schedule to ascertain their views on child and family matters (The Family Interview Schedule 1; C. McAuley, unpublished questionnaire). Following that, they were asked to complete a number of measures on the same subject areas. Finally they completed the economic questionnaire (an adapted version of the Client Service Receipt Inventory; Beecham and Knapp, 2001).

At the follow-up interviews approximately 1 year later, the mothers were again interviewed in their own homes by the same researchers. The format was similar to that of the initial interviews. A follow-up interview on child and family matters was completed with the mothers (The Family

Interview Schedule 2; C. McAuley and N. McCurry, unpublished questionnaire). Following that, they were asked to complete the same child welfare quantitative measures and economic questionnaire as at the baseline interview. An additional questionnaire on the costs of Home-Start (Service Receipt Inventory; M. Knapp *et al.*, unpublished questionnaire) was completed by the participating Home-Start schemes.

Child welfare outcomes

The child welfare aspects of the study were designed specifically to examine change in selected outcome domains (areas) over time. It was planned that two avenues should be used to explore this: interviews with the mothers and results from outcome measures. Hence the interview content with the mothers and the measures they were asked to complete were directly related. The interviews with the mothers addressed five core areas:

- the stresses related to parenting young children

- maternal mental health

- maternal self-esteem

- emotional and social development of the children

- maternal social support.

The measures completed by the mothers addressed the outcome domains as follows.

- Parenting stress: the Parenting Stress Index (Abidin, 1995).

- Maternal mental health: the Edinburgh Postnatal Depression Scale (Cox *et al.*, 1987) and the Centre for Epidemiological Studies Depression Scale (Radloff, 1977).

- Maternal self-esteem: the Rosenberg Self-Esteem Scale (Rosenberg, 1965).

- Emotional and social development of the children: the Brief Infant–Toddler Social and Emotional Assessment Scale (Briggs-Gowan and Carter, 2001).

- Maternal social support: the Maternal Social Support Index (Pascoe *et al.*, 1988).

An overview of the measures is provided in Table 1. Further details of the measures can be found in Appendix 2.

Summary

The recent green paper *Every Child Matters* (DfES, 2003) indicates the government's intention to place support for parents and carers at the centre of its approach to improving children's lives. It has been recognised for some time, however, that services such as family support should be offered where needs have been assessed and where there is a likelihood of beneficial outcomes for children and families. More recently there is an expectation that such services should also be seen to be good value for money. Hence it has become imperative for commissioners and providers to produce evidence of effectiveness and cost-effectiveness.

Evaluating community-based initiatives to support children and their families has proved challenging. A particular dilemma has been how to maintain scientific rigour while facing ethical and practical constraints of conducting research with families in need. Outcome measurement in child welfare is also a highly complex area, and providing tangible outcome measures for family support initiatives has proved challenging. Home-Start is a large and long-established voluntary organisation offering family support throughout the UK and in many other countries. It offers support through the use of volunteers and it is predominantly offered through home visiting. Previous research on Home-Start has found high levels of parent satisfaction with the service.

The aim of this study was to evaluate the outcomes and costs of Home-Start support to young families experiencing stress. It was confined to stresses experienced by families who were referred as a result of maternal mental/physical health, social isolation, multiple births/young children and a child/children with special needs. Two groups of mothers participated: 80 Study families who were in receipt of Home-Start support and 82 Comparison families who were not. Both groups were drawn from south-east England and Northern Ireland. All the families were interviewed at the outset of the study and 1 year later. The families completed a semi-structured interview and measures related to child and family well-being, as well as an economic questionnaire, at both time points.

In the following chapters, we introduce the families as well as exploring the mothers' views and needs at the outset of the study. We then move on to examining their views 1 year later and the outcomes at that stage. The economic situation of the families and their receipt of services over time are also provided. The cost-effectiveness of Home-Start is also addressed. The concluding chapter summarises the key findings of the study.

2 The families at outset

Introduction

In this chapter, we describe the characteristics of the young families at the time of first-stage interviews. We were primarily comparing two groups: mothers who were in receipt of Home-Start support (Study) and mothers who were not (Comparison). As this was an effectiveness/cost-effectiveness study, it was also important to examine the extent to which the two groups of mothers were similar. Hence in this chapter we explore a number of factors relating to the mothers, their children and their husbands/partners. A case study is also provided for illustration. Given that the sample was drawn from both Northern Ireland and south-east England, regional differences were also explored. Where significant differences were found, they are included. The information provided in this chapter was collected during face-to-face interviews with mothers using the Family Information Schedule (C. McAuley, unpublished questionnaire) and the Client Service Receipt Inventory (Beecham and Knapp, 2001).

Mothers and their children

One-hundred and sixty-two families took part in both the initial and follow-up interviews and completed the measures. Of those mothers, 80 (49.4 per cent) were supported by Home-Start (Study) and 82 (50.6 per cent) were in the Comparison group. A higher proportion of families (60 per cent Study; 54 per cent Comparison) lived in Northern Ireland (Figure 1). Only one mother was not of white ethnic origin, describing herself as Black Caribbean. This was not surprising as Home-Start's figures for the referral period of the study in these areas indicated that it was predominantly (90 per cent English referrals; 98 per cent Northern Ireland referrals) serving a white British population (*Home-Start Ethnic Monitoring Report 2000–01*; Home-Start, personal communication).

We had initially recruited a further 15 families. However, at follow-up they either could not be contacted or chose not to participate. The 15

Figure 1 Number of families by group and region

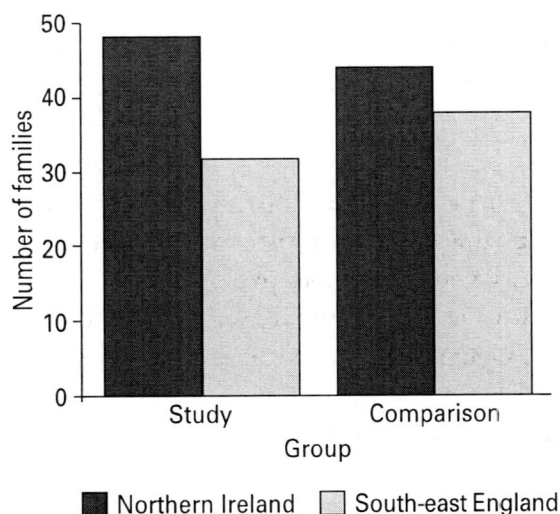

families that were excluded did not differ from those that were retained regarding any of the main family characteristics/maternal and child well-being variables. All analyses throughout this report relate to the sample of 162 families.

Mothers' ages ranged from 17 to 42 years old, the average for both groups being 30 years. However, eight mothers (5 per cent) were 20 years or younger. Around two-thirds of the mothers were living with their husbands or partners, while single mothers headed the other 51 households.

Children living in the household

The average number of children per family household was three, although the number varied from one to six. There was a significant difference between family size in Northern Ireland and south-east England, with the former generally having a larger number of children (Figure 2). Twenty-three families (14.2 per cent) had had multiple births. All of these were twins, apart from one family who had triplets and another with two sets of twins. More than four-fifths of families had one or two children under 5 years of age. The remaining 27 families had between three and five children of that age. Almost half had a child of 1 year or younger, while almost a third had a child of 6 months or younger.

Figure 2 Number of families and children by region

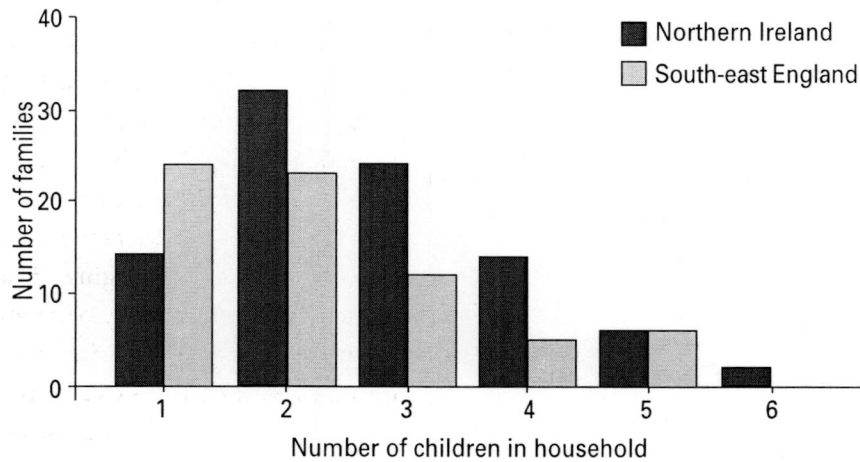

Children with special needs

All mothers were asked if they considered their children to have any special needs regarding any aspect of their children's health and/or development. The definition used for special needs was if the mother thought that the child required additional parental attention and/or support as a result of health and/or developmental problems. However, it was clear from the responses that some mothers had taken into account a diagnosis or classification of their child's special needs as a result of contacts with health/social care professionals. There was a wide range of special needs reported (Table 2). Examples included attention deficit hyperactivity disorder (ADHD), speech problems and autism. Using this broad definition, more than half (87) of the mothers indicated that they had one or more children with special needs and 23 mothers had two or three children with these needs.

Table 2 Most frequently cited special needs of children at baseline

Special need	Frequency
Speech problems	26
Behavioural problems	25
Hearing difficulties	15
Physical development problems	11
Asthma	11
Cognitive development problems	10
Emotional and social development problems	10
Heart problems	8
ADHD	8
Premature birth-related health/ development problems	7
Dyspraxia	6
Eczema	5
Autism	5
Epilepsy	3
Enuresis	3
Physical co-ordination problems	3
Hyperactivity	3

Housing

About half of all the families were living in owner-occupied homes, a quarter in homes rented from the council or the Northern Ireland Housing Executive (NIHE), 14 per cent in privately rented accommodation and 7 per cent in housing association accommodation. The Comparison group had significantly fewer families living in owner-occupied homes and more families renting from the council or NIHE than the Home-Start group.

On average, there were three bedrooms per household. A few families were living in very overcrowded conditions: one family of two adults and six children was in a three-bedroom accommodation, although three of the children were very young triplets. Another family of two adults and four children was living in a one-bedroom house, and a third family of two adults and five children was in a very small two-bedroom house.

Income and employment

Families were asked to indicate their main source of income, although they did not necessarily rely solely on that one source. Earnings were the main source for more than half the sample, but 85 per cent of single-parent families (who comprised one-third of the sample) relied mainly on social security benefits. Mothers were asked to indicate their weekly household income using bands of £100. More than three-quarters of the families were receiving less than £300 per week from their main source of income: commonly £101–£200.

Two-thirds of the mothers remained at home to look after the children and had no paid employment. About a quarter were employed either full- or part-time. About half of the working mothers had managerial or professional positions, or were working in the service sector (such as teaching or catering). Mothers in full-time employment worked an average of 38 hours per week, while the mean for those in part-time employment was 16 hours.

On average, and excluding annual leave, employed mothers had taken 42 days off work in the previous 3 months (out of a possible 60 working days), although much of this was maternity leave (58 per cent of mothers).

The mothers' partners were almost all in full-time employment, averaging 45 hours per week, and took many fewer days off work than the group of mothers (on average 1 day per month). Although few employed partners experienced work difficulties because of family stresses, a few did have significant lengths of time off work, usually to provide additional support at home. Two partners were unable to work as they needed to look after children because of the mother's mental health problems or physical disability.

Service-use patterns

We asked mothers about their use of services over the previous 3 months (and use of hospital inpatient services over 12 months). Case study A illustrates the complexity of one family's needs and the services it was using. In Chapter 7 we look at service-use changes over time, and at that point provide some further details on the baseline service-use patterns described below.

> **Case study: family A**
> Both parents lived with their five children in a two-bedroom rented flat. The mother, a part-time student, found coping with five children very difficult in such a small space. The youngest child had several allergies and saw a specialist nurse every month. One child had learning disabilities and attended a special needs school. He also had problems with his hearing and many chest infections. The middle child (age 11) had behavioural problems for
> *(Continued overleaf)*

which he took medication. He had a number of psychiatric, counselling and paediatric supports and attended a child guidance clinic. The eldest child had been in trouble with the police. The family's considerable health problems meant they saw a GP almost twice a week. They also had support from a social worker, lawyer and doctor. A voluntary organisation helped them get disability living allowance for the middle child.

At the baseline interview, the mother's self-esteem was low and she felt she was not coping very well. She had eczema and asthma and thought she may be having a recurrence of last year's depression. She received quite a lot of support from her partner (who had taken 6 days off work to help at home), her mother and a friend, but felt that 'someone to talk to would be really nice ... when you need to ... without being critical ... who understands the situation but who could be objective'. Such complex family scenarios are not uncommon for Home-Start volunteers.

Education and day care

The families in the study were young families, many without school-age children, just under half with one or more children in primary school, and only a tenth with children in middle or secondary school. Children in six families were attending special schools, and some others were receiving extra lessons (6 per cent of families) or attending after-school clubs (9 per cent). Two very young children with developmental delay were receiving home support from the Portage Early Education Support Service. Only 27 families reported using some kind of day care for preschool children (childminder, regular support from family, crèche, nanny, respite carer), and 34 families had children attending mother and toddler groups (commonly twice a week).

Overnight services

The most common reason for children being away overnight was regular contact visits with family (usually non-cohabiting fathers or grandparents) or friends. Children in 13 families (8 per cent) had an average of 17 nights away over the 3 months. Children's homes and boarding schools had not been used. Foster care was only used by children in one family: four children stayed for a week, and one child with severe behavioural difficulties stayed for 3 weeks. One mother and child spent a month in a women's aid hostel.

Hospital services

Overnight stays in hospital were quite common: 70 per cent of families had at least one person admitted during the year before baseline interviews. The most common reason was for maternity reasons, but in a third of cases a child was admitted to a paediatric ward or to a special care baby unit. Psychiatric or general healthcare admissions were rare. Families in the Comparison group spent significantly fewer days in hospital (5 days) than Study group families (15 days).

Accident and emergency (A&E) attendance rates were quite high by national standards (all children), with about a third of mothers reporting at least one attendance in 3 months, attending on average 1.3 times. Four people, all from the Comparison group, used an ambulance. Fourteen families had used day hospital, in two cases to give birth.

Nearly two-thirds of all the families had had at least one hospital outpatient appointment in the last 3 months. The average was one appointment per month. The most common reasons were paediatric appointments, physiotherapy, check-ups or scans to monitor particular conditions, counselling, eye checks, psychiatry and antenatal appointments.

Community health services

Almost all families (94 per cent) had contact with a health visitor in the 3 months before the baseline interview, usually in their own homes, with an average of four contacts, each lasting around 40 minutes. Similarly, almost every family (95 per cent) had contact with a general practitioner (GP). The average number of GP contacts per family was eight, half of them at the surgery. Appointments lasted about 12 minutes. Again these were quite high figures by national standards. The Comparison group had significantly fewer home contacts with a GP (mean 0.10) than the Home-Start group (mean 0.35). One in seven of the mothers interviewed had been in contact with a midwife, mostly in the family home, occurring about once a fortnight.

One child had had contact with a speech therapist at home, but all other speech therapy (involving 20 children) was either at a clinic or school. On average, two speech therapy sessions of 45 minutes were received each month. Around 10 per cent of the families had used a complementary therapy: the most common were aromatherapy, massage and homeopathy. Other community-based health services included dentist, optician, vaccination, orthodontist, child development centre, child guidance unit, family centre, methadone programme, community nurse, junior opportunities group for children with developmental delay, podiatrist, community-based physiotherapy, gynaecologist, paediatrician, occupational therapy, well woman clinic and baby clinic.

Mental health services

About a third of the families had used mental health services, with 13 per cent in contact with a community psychiatric nurse (CPN), averaging four visits over the 3 months, to treat the mother's mental health problems. Most other mental health service contacts were for individual counselling or therapy for mothers. Four children had seen a child psychologist for behavioural or developmental problems, and four children with learning difficulties had seen an educational psychologist.

Care, support and advice

Support from home care workers depended on availability and local policies: the majority of the 11 per cent of families receiving this service were in the Northern Ireland Study group, and usually saw a care worker twice a week for about 2 hours each visit. Almost a fifth of all families had contact with a social worker. Few other support services were used, and by few families. These included parenting skills training groups, family support workers, women's refuge, telephone help lines, various parent support groups, holiday schemes, Citizens Advice Bureau and housing officers.

As many as a quarter of the families had had contact with a solicitor in the previous 3 months, most commonly for purchasing property, writing wills, child protection cases and to place injunction orders on abusive ex-partners. Only 10 per cent of families had had contact with the police; six families had had a member who had appeared in court (for domestic violence, custody of children, injunction orders and housing and social security benefit issues).

Partners' service use

We asked mothers with partners about their partner's use of services. Half had not used any services at all in the 3-month period, a quarter had seen a GP and a fifth had been to a dentist. A&E attendance was quite high (10 per cent), a similar proportion had used other outpatient services, and three partners had stayed overnight in hospital. Other services used included counselling, community nurse, CPN, methadone programme, Citizens Advice Bureau, housing officer, solicitor and a child custody case conference.

Summary

One-hundred and sixty-two families took part in the study. The average number of children per household was three. Almost half of the families had a child of 1 year or less. Mote than half of the mothers described their children as having special needs. Two-thirds of the mothers were living with partners. Most mothers were not in paid employment, while most partners were working. Just over half of the families lived in rented accommodation. Income levels were low, and most of the single-parent families relied mainly on social security benefits.

There were no significant differences found between the Study and Comparison groups regarding age of the mothers, lone parenthood, number and age of children, number of children with special needs, multiple births and ethnic origin. The one significant difference between families in Northern Ireland and south-east England was the greater number of children in the former.

The families used a range of services. Many of the mothers had recently had a new baby, and all families had young children. Contact with mental health services, A&E and GPs was quite high. Again there were few differences between the Study and Comparison groups: the main difference was in inpatient service use, where the proportion of families using the services was no different but mean length of stay was significantly greater for the Study group. Many inpatient stays were maternity-related, and lengths of stay for this reason were noticeably longer for mothers in our sample (7.6 days for Study group, 5.0 days for Comparison group) compared with the national average (2.1 days) (Office of National Statistics, 2001).

Overall, therefore, the Study and Comparison group families were quite well matched.

3 Mothers' perspectives at outset

Introduction

In this chapter we summarise views on the stresses the mothers were experiencing as parents at the time of the first-stage interviews. Their perceptions of their self-esteem, their children's well-being and their support needs are described in detail. The initial impressions of the Study group's mothers on Home-Start are also provided. Two case studies are included for illustration.

Parenting stress

All of the mothers (Study and Comparison) were asked about the current stresses they were experiencing as parents of young children. The majority identified multiple factors affecting their parenting at that time. The average number was six (Figure 3 and Table 3). Both groups of mothers identified similar factors, the eight most frequently identified being identical for both groups. Maternal mental health, isolation and lack of support and the sense of being overwhelmed by the many demands of young dependent children were the most often cited.

Figure 3 Number of stresses identified by mothers at baseline

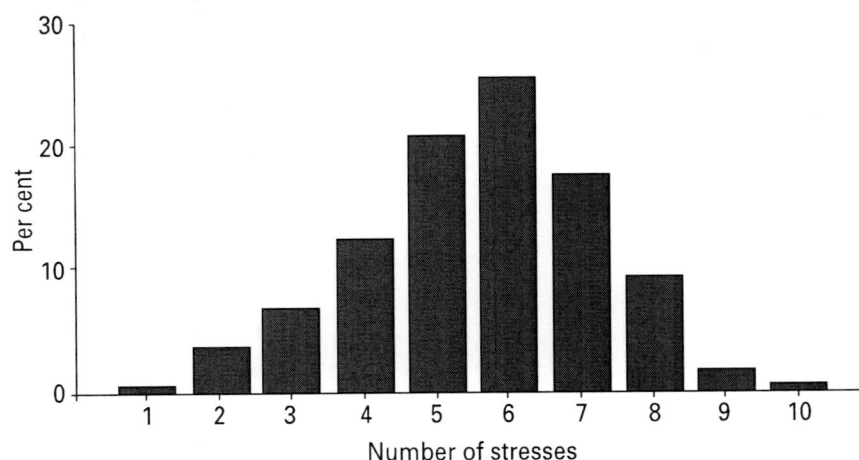

Table 3 Most frequently identified stress factors reported by mothers at baseline (by rank order)

No. of times stress factor identified by Study mothers	Stress factors	No. of times stress factor identified by Comparison mothers
64	Mothers' mental health	67
78	Lack of support/isolation	64
64	Multiple demands/no time for self	43
39	Financial	37
32	Parenting issues and child behaviour problems	37
31	Children with special needs	32
27	Mothers' physical health/disability	34
20	Wider family issues	28

Case study: Study family B at baseline

At baseline interview this mother had two children, aged 8 years and 3 years, and was living with her husband. She had recently left full-time employment in human resources due to mental illness.

At the time of interview the mother was experiencing multiple stresses, several of which were specifically related to mental health. She had suffered from postnatal depression since the birth of the last baby and was on medication. Additionally, she also experienced periods of anxiety and almost daily panic attacks. In the previous 12 months she had spent a short period in a psychiatric hospital as a result of feeling suicidal. She was isolated and lonely, as she was not from the area in which she now lived. Moreover, she had taken time off work to look after her children and was worried about the financial implications of not being in paid employment. She and her husband were owner-occupiers of a three-bedroom house and their main source of income was now the husband's earnings, which ranged between £300 and £400 per week. She was also concerned about her son who was displaying behaviour problems. As a result of her mental health, her husband was worried about leaving her alone in the house.

At the time of the first interview the mother's sister and mother offered emotional support, while her mother-in-law provided practical support and respite. She indicated that she would welcome more people to turn to for practical support and advice on parenting skills. Having read about Home-Start in the library she referred herself. Her volunteer had been visiting for a few weeks. She hoped that the Home-Start volunteer would befriend her and provide emotional support.

Case study: Comparison family C at baseline

At baseline interview this mother was a lone parent with four children, aged 7, 6, 4 and 2 years. Three of her children were in primary school while the youngest attended day nursery.

This mother was experiencing stress as a result of several interconnected factors. She described how she was under extreme financial pressure. She lived in rented accommodation and her main source of income was social security benefits, which ranged from £100 to £200 per week. She was finding it difficult to meet the demands of her four children and give them all adequate attention. Moreover, she described feeling depressed and was experiencing sleep problems. She had recently been assaulted and as a consequence was on medication to reduce anxiety. There was a pending court case connected with the assault that was causing her a lot of concern. She was worried about her son, who had learning and speech difficulties and was withdrawn from other children.

At the time of the first interview this mother indicated that she would turn to her friend, family and health visitor for support and respite, someone to talk to and someone to take the children out. She would have welcomed more people to turn to for support, particularly someone who could share parenting experiences with her.

Emergent themes from the mothers' interviews

To help us understand more about the difficulties the families faced, we selected all 42 families who were experiencing the average (six) number of stresses. The stresses these families were facing were typical of those experienced in the wider sample. A number of core themes emerged and these are described in detail below.

Pregnancy/birth trauma and mothers' well-being postbirth

From the interviews, it was apparent that pregnancy had a lot of important repercussions for the mothers. A considerable number of the mothers experienced severe health problems and trauma directly associated with pregnancy and birth. Sometimes this was in regard to the most recently born child, but at other times it was with regard to an older child or even the birth of every one of a mother's children. Furthermore, a significant number of these mothers experienced postnatal depression either following the birth of their youngest child or following the birth of a number of their children. The pregnancies also resulted in wider and significant changes in the lives of these mothers.

> It was … 11 hours in labour and then it turned out to be an emergency Caesarean … I was sort of happy to leave the hospital, then when I got home I was scared. I had nobody to turn to.

> Trying to recover from an operation and then trying to work with a newborn baby. Well, there's the night feeds and … after an operation you're tired anyway … I think part of it was exhaustion.

Transition to parenthood

What came across from these interviews, and in particular from the mothers expressing most distress, was a picture of families entering a rapid downward spiral as a result of an accumulation of stress factors on the family unit over a relatively short period. As indicated above, very often these mothers had experienced ill health during the pregnancy and birth and began parenthood with considerable physical and mental health problems.

Sleep deprivation was frequently mentioned as a serious problem, and not only for the early weeks of a baby's life. In some families, sleep deprivation lasted for up to a year. While the addition of a new baby obviously had an impact on all of the families, what was striking was the description of the huge adaptation needed by first-time mothers and their husband/partners. Developing effective communication in the early stages of parenthood seemed crucial.

> You know, he's never slept … It's hard, sitting up here all night and then they're getting up and it's just … no sleep

> He [husband] is more supportive now because I've sat down and I've been really honest with him and said 'listen, I can't cope'.

Perhaps one of the most worrying aspects was the fact that many of these mothers were also isolated. This isolation might have been the result of moving into a new area where they did not have a network of friends and family, having estranged relationships with family, being depressed or anxious about leaving the family home, having no transport or not being able to drive, or living in an area where there was either no facilities to meet other mothers and toddlers or it was difficult to obtain information about facilities. There was a widespread sense of these mothers having lost their freedom, through the responsibilities of parenting young children. They frequently expressed a sense of loss of personal identity. They perceived their only role in life to be that of a mother. They appeared to have considerably low self-esteem and there was a strong sense of a feeling of loss of control over their lives.

I don't see anybody as such through the day … Now I'm spending the majority of my time with children, having no … adult communication.

It's just … I need time by myself. I'm always Mum … I'm not me anymore.

Many of these mothers had had to give up their jobs. It was evident that the loss of their job brought a loss of status as a wage earner within society as well as within their own family. There was also the loss of adult company through employment in addition to the loss of financial independence.

When we just had the one child I still worked part time and I had quite a well-paid job. And now we have lost that.

That's why I miss work … having the adult company.

Multiple demands of young children on one adult

Across all the sample of mothers, the stress related to the constancy of demands of young dependent children was a recurrent theme. The mothers described in graphic details the problems of 'juggling' the needs of their children with managing a household on a daily basis. Whether the mothers were first time or experienced, they expressed considerable difficulty in managing their time to meet the needs of their children.

You're on the go from morning to night, 24 hours a day, 7 days a week.

Mothers who already had children stressed the difficulty of simultaneously meeting the differing needs of new babies and older children.

The issue is having the age gap … you get through one round of feeding … but then you have somebody else who has totally different needs.

Often many of these mothers were the sole carers for these young children on a daily basis. It is not surprising then that the need for respite should be a central concern for them.

I don't get any break at all. Not even at night because they don't sleep.

Lack of available support and need for respite

The mothers highlighted a need for practical and/or emotional support. The daily child-care support they most wanted was respite to allow them to manage the household and meet their own needs. Generally these mothers lacked support from their own or their husbands'/partners' extended family. Usually it was as a result of their families living a considerable distance away from them or the mothers having estranged relations with their families.

I haven't got anyone really down here that I can speak to. I love my kids to bits and I wouldn't be without them, but I need a break at the same time … I just … feel so alone …

Mothers' mental health

There was widespread evidence of mothers having depressive symptoms despite the fact that only 19 of this subgroup were referred for mental health problems. The mothers described symptoms of feeling confused, forgetful, loss of energy and anxiety/panic attacks as well as feeling despondent. Often they felt overwhelmed and unable to cope. They described mood swings, negative thinking and the inability to trust others.

The most frequently mentioned form of depression was postnatal depression. As referred to earlier, some of the mothers were experiencing this for the first time after the birth of their most recent/first baby; some had experienced it since the birth of an earlier child some time ago and one mother had experienced it after the birth of every child. In some cases these mothers had a history of depression in their younger lives, but in others there was no history of mental health problems. Often it followed birth trauma and maternal physical health problems. There were a few descriptions of mothers having difficulty bonding with their babies after birth.

I went through labour all day ... and they kept losing P's [baby's] heartbeat ... and they had to give me an emergency Caesarean section ... then I had a lot of infections ... and then I just got ... postnatal depression.

When ... it was first diagnosed ... I didn't feel close to him. I didn't have any feelings towards him ... it was just like, you know, a chore.

There was some evidence of mothers having struggled with postnatal depression for several months after birth before a diagnosis was made by any of the professionals concerned. However, when the diagnosis was made it appeared that considerable efforts had been made to mobilise resources to support the mother. This support generally took the form of the prescription of anti-depressants and regular visiting by a community psychiatric nurse. In some cases there was evidence of direct involvement of a psychiatrist. A few mothers also received the services of a counsellor. One important final point raised by mothers was their inability to attend postnatal support groups due to the fact that there were no facilities for looking after their young children.

They had offered ... postnatal groups ... but you weren't allowed to take the kids with you, so that was no good to me cause I had nobody to keep them.

On the whole, most of the mothers with mental health problems appeared to be experiencing them at a moderate to severe level. Many were on long-term medication. Some of these mothers had been admitted for lengthy periods to psychiatric hospitals in recent years. A small number had attempted or considered suicide in the recent past.

There was some evidence that the mothers were aware of and concerned about the impact of their mental health problems on their husbands/partners and their children. Some mothers indicated that they recognised that they were more quick-tempered than usual with both their husbands/partners and children. Others expressed concern about the lack of opportunities the children had to get out of the house when they felt unable to do so.

All I do is cry. I'm short-tempered with the kids, I wouldn't harm them, but I snap at them. And ... I also snap at my husband as well.

Several of the mothers spoke of unresolved loss relating to earlier miscarriages, death of significant family figures or as a result of a marriage/partnership break-up. There was certainly a sense that these unresolved feelings had contributed to the mothers' mental health problems.

I was devastated, I'm still devastated. I went for a check-up, because I couldn't feel the baby moving anymore and they told me that he'd died. Everybody expected me just to forget about it and get on with it.

Many of the mothers with significant mental health problems were also often isolated. They were attempting to cope with the multiple demands of young dependent children, in the context of little available support from husbands/partners or wider families.

Parenting a child/children with special needs and/or behavioural problems

Parenting young dependent children became even more demanding where one or more of the children had special needs or significant behaviour problems. The range of special needs of the children was considerably wide. In many cases, the concerns were problems with the physical health/development of babies and young children. However, it also included a considerable number of children with emotional and behavioural problems and developmental delay. Many mothers expressed concern about speech and language development. A smaller number of children had been diagnosed as having conditions such as ADHD or Asperger's syndrome. Some mothers had one child with special needs while others were caring for several.

Some mothers were caring for one child with highly complex special needs.

> *I don't think he has behaviour problems, but he's been having a lot of tantrums, he's been biting and he's been violent to me and his sister ... It makes it very stressful when we go out because he has tantrums and is badly behaved.*

Mothers who indicated that their children had behaviour problems expressed considerable frustration in managing their behaviour. Mothers of the children with special needs, including behaviour problems, often expressed concern about the impact of these children's needs on their siblings.

A major issue for all of these mothers was the length of time taken to reach a diagnosis of the children's special needs. In some cases this appeared to take several years. The mothers clearly indicated that having a diagnosis helped them in some way to deal with the problem. Several of the mothers indicated that they felt professionals did not take their concerns seriously enough initially and they related this to the delay in reaching a diagnosis. One mother poignantly described how diagnosis brought relief at the same time as the end of hope.

> *Very mixed feelings ... I was relieved that I wasn't going mad and that there was an explanation. But, at the same time, I felt that the hope that it was just a phase had been taken away.*

Another particular factor causing stress for these mothers was the need to attend multiple specialist appointments for these children in different locations. Understandably this posed particular problems as many of the mothers lacked available transport or simply found it almost impossible to travel with multiple young children including the children with special needs. Again, some mothers indicated that they were not able to attend some medical appointments simply due to the fact that they had no available support to mind their other children.

Mothers' physical health/disability

Several mothers had a physical disability or were experiencing physical health problems. Two mothers in this sample were registered blind. Some of the physical health problems appeared to be related to pregnancy / birth or postbirth complications. A few mothers related other health problems, such as hair loss, directly to their experience of stress. Other health issues mentioned included gallbladder problems and underactive thyroid glands. Many mothers were concerned about weight gain.

Financial worries

Many of the mothers were in employment prior to giving birth. As a result, they faced the major decision of whether to return to or leave work. For most mothers, the financial implications of parenthood appeared to restrict the number of options that they had. Some mothers in partnerships thought their only option was to return to work to ensure two salaries to cover the existing mortgage and increased household costs. Others thought that they should give up work to care for their children as a result of being unable to meet the costs of alternative child care. Many mothers were highly critical of the lack of alternative child-care provision, which was deemed to be inaccessible to them.

> *There is no support network like cheaper crèche facilities ... if you want to do ... part time work.*

Some mothers expressed difficulty in living on benefits from week to week. They expressed anxiety about not meeting their children's needs, indicating that they could only afford the basics and were not able to give their children treats or take them on holidays. Many mothers worried how they were going to pay the bills and a couple of mothers reported that they were in debt.

Mothers' relationship with ex-husbands/ex-partners

A large number of mothers in this sample faced problems with their ex-husbands/ex-partners over access to and financial arrangements for their children. Some mothers had the added stress of awaiting court cases to help resolve these issues. A few of the mothers reported that they had experienced domestic violence when living with their husband/partner. A larger number indicated that they were still dealing with aggression and bullying in their contacts with their ex-husbands/ex-partners on these matters. More generally, it was obvious that the mothers were still coping with their own emotional adjustment to the situation and attempting to overcome hurt and sadness. They also had to deal with their children's reactions to the separation from their fathers/father figures. In most cases the parents were concerned about disturbance of the children's routines and inconsistency in parenting.

> He [husband] *will ring up and just give me a load of abuse over the phone ... about once every week...he* [son] *is always asking to see his dad ... but he's worse when he has spoken to his dad on the phone...he's just really boisterous then.*

Mothers' self-esteem

Around half of the mothers in the entire sample described themselves as having low self-esteem. Slightly more of the mothers in the Study group reported this than in the Comparison group. More than a quarter of the rest of the mothers in the entire sample estimated that their self-esteem was fine, and 15 of the mothers rated their self-esteem as good or high. Fairly similar proportions of the Study and Comparison mothers categorised themselves in this way.

Mothers who indicated they had low self-esteem
A number of core factors appeared to be associated with the low self-esteem of mothers. One major contributing factor appeared to be the mothers'

perceived inability to cope. A few described themselves as feeling deficient as mothers. Others were critical of their ability to manage their young children and their households.

> *You don't have much time for yourself ... so after a while you just feel that you're not coping ... that just gradually gets you down.*

Many of the mothers indicated that their physical appearance in general, and weight gain in particular, contributed a great deal to how they perceived themselves.

> *And going about constantly dressed in the cheapest clothes and constantly wear my hair tied back ... I just feel, you know, really ugly.*

Some mothers described a sense of loss of their personal identity. They saw themselves solely now as in the role of mothers. They found it difficult to have any time for themselves, concentrating solely on children/families and neglecting their own needs.

> *I just feel like ... I've got no life of my own. Everything I do is for them ... for the children and my husband.*

Other mothers thought that their low self-esteem was associated with isolation. They were unable to leave the house as a result of the practical difficulties of taking multiple young children outside the home or due to their lack of confidence or mental health difficulties.

> *I need to go to more groups and meet more people. I need to get some more friends. Cause I do isolate myself, and that doesn't help my self-esteem at all.*

Finally, some mothers thought that the fact that they were no longer in employment had affected their self-confidence.

> *I just have no confidence in myself anymore at all. Like, I used to be very confident. Now I would just say hello ... and walk on ... Because ... what have I got to talk about?*

Mothers who indicated their self-esteem was fine
These mothers were characterised by fluctuations in how they saw themselves as parents. In other words, some days they felt confident and they were doing the best for their children, while on other days they felt the opposite. One mother interestingly commented on the lack of feedback and support that a parent receives in contrast to someone in paid employment.

Mothers who indicated they had high self-esteem
In stark contrast to those mothers with low self-esteem, the accounts of this small group of mothers highlighted the joy and fun they experienced with their children, which appeared to balance the more stressful and difficult times. There was a strong sense of the mothers' pride in achieving motherhood. Equally there was a strong sense of achievement related to the babies' developmental progress. Furthermore there were indications that these mothers' identity had not been threatened by motherhood and they indeed described themselves as happy in themselves and motherhood as having given them something more to look forward to in life.

> *For all the hard work ... it's definitely worth it. For all the stresses that are involved, we have lots of fun with them. We get lots of enjoyment from all of them ... from the three of them ... and I would say that we are very happy.*

> *I think because I take a sort of pride, I suppose, in the fact that I managed to carry the twins to 39 weeks and then have my planned Caesarean. And I'm breastfeeding and I'm succeeding in doing that ... and the kids are happy. And for me, that makes me feel good because I'm achieving something.*

Children's well-being
Each mother interviewed was asked to select the child she was most concerned about (if any) in respect of each of the following aspects of development: behaviour, language, social–emotional, physical and cognitive. The children chosen were also the subject for the PSI/SF and BITSEA measures. Almost three-quarters of the mothers in the overall sample identified some concerns about at least one aspect of the selected children's development. Most of these mothers had concerns across two to four areas of development. Some only had concerns about one area of the children's development. However, a small number had concerns about their children across all areas of development. This group of children was characterised by diagnoses of severe health/developmental problems. The group included children with autism, ADHD, learning difficulties, a rare condition called XLAG, a brain cyst and microcephaly.

Social support
On the whole both groups of mothers appeared to have few people available for support. The most frequently cited providers of support were families, friends, neighbours, health visitors and GPs. Both groups of mothers predominantly turned to family members. The mothers in both the Study and Comparison groups received practical, emotional and financial support as well as advice from these people. Not surprisingly, the vast majority of the mothers in both groups indicated that they would welcome more people for support. They sought further services, in particular crèche facilities for respite, further emotional and practical support, and information and advice on parenting young children, especially those with special needs.

> *A wee crèche even for a couple of hours, you know ... for babies of that age ... that isn't going to cost an arm and a leg basically.*

> *That's what I want ... someone that can just come in and out and ... form a relationship with them.*

Home-Start support
Finally, all the Study mothers at the time of first interview had been receiving Home-Start support

for a few weeks. The vast majority of the mothers had originally heard about Home-Start from their health visitors. The remainder had heard about it from friends, advertisements, other professionals (GPs, social services, midwives, psychiatric nurses) family members or other voluntary organisations. They were often seeking someone to take care of the children while they completed other tasks and someone to accompany them to appointments or family outings.

I know she will take him to the park and I can get my housework done. It is nice to have that couple of hours to have a break.

Some mothers were isolated and wanted adult company, a friend or simply to get out more.

Somebody to sit down and have a chat with, a cup of coffee, go up the town for a walk. I think it's just generally having somebody there to listen to you.

Mothers appreciated the fact that the volunteers would have had experience with children and welcomed their advice and knowledge.

I think it's because they've got experience with children, and I wanted more support. When I was told about it I thought it sounded just right.

Some mothers accepted Home-Start as a direct result of having recognised that they could no longer cope with the responsibilities of caring for young dependent children without further support. However, in a considerable number of situations there was very little evidence that the mothers were offered any alternative service to consider. In some situations the mothers reported feeling pressurised to accept the service due to the concern of professionals about the well-being of themselves or their children.

Really at the time when I was referred, I was just taking any help that was offered because I was in such a bad way.

Pressure from the health visitor and the GP ... The only reason I accepted it was because they were telling me that I was down ... that I couldn't cope.

Expectations of Home-Start

Mothers were asked what they expected of their Home-Start volunteers. For the majority of mothers their expectations fell into three main areas: help with their children; having someone to talk to and listen to them; having a friend.

The majority of mothers in the study expected their volunteers to play with the children, spend time with/occupy the children, or help with their children. This would allow the mothers to engage in other tasks within the house, have a lie down, have a bath or shower, or simply provide the mothers with some respite from caring for their children. In both groups, respite from caring for their children was the most frequently noted expectation of the majority of the mothers. The majority of mothers also wanted someone to talk to and listen to them and many of them also wanted the volunteers to be their friends. Many of the mothers expected practical assistance in taking themselves and their children to medical appointments, the post office or shopping; practical support was expected with family outings and supporting the mothers to widen their social networks in the local community. Some mothers expected advice on parenting from the volunteers.

It is also important to add that a few of the mothers indicated that they had no expectations at all and, perhaps more worryingly, did not seem to feel that they had any right to place any expectations on the volunteers simply because they were there on a voluntary basis. Finally, some mothers commented on the duration and frequency of the home visits.

Thinking about Home-Start, that is a great help. Just something like that, but a little more frequently ... so if someone can come for ... even if it was just twice a week ... that would be a great help.

Summary

In summary, from these interviews we have a picture of mothers who were under considerable stress that affected their parenting capacity. The stresses they were experiencing were multiple and related to different aspects of their family lives. Many of these mothers had experienced considerable trauma associated with the pregnancy and birth of their children and this was affecting their well-being at the time of the interviews. There was a strong sense of these mothers at times being overwhelmed by the amount of demands being placed upon them by caring for multiple children of different developmental ages. What seemed to make the situation extremely stressful for most mothers was the lack of respite.

There was widespread evidence of depressive symptoms among these mothers beyond those who had been referred for this reason. The most frequently cited form of depression was postnatal depression. Generally, most of the mothers with mental health problems were experiencing them at a moderate to severe level. Many of these mothers attempting to care for several young dependent children were also isolated.

Almost three-quarters of the mothers identified some concerns about their children's development.

A major concern for these mothers was the length of time taken to reach a diagnosis of their children's special needs. Another related factor causing stress was the need to attend multiple specialist appointments in different locations often many miles away from their homes. Particular problems posed included travelling alone with several young children and availability of transport.

Many of the mothers expressed concerns about their financial situation. Most had been in employment prior to giving birth. Often they were in a dilemma as to whether to return to work or not. Many were highly critical of the lack of affordable and accessible child-care facilities in their areas. Many mothers faced problems with their ex-husbands/ex-partners over access to and financial arrangements for their children.

Given all these stressful factors, it was particularly unfortunate that many mothers indicated that they had little available support. The vast majority of all the mothers indicated that they would welcome more people to turn to for support. The Study mothers had been receiving Home-Start support for a few weeks at the time of these interviews. They had not received this support before; most had heard about it from their health visitors. Their expectations were for practical and emotional support.

4 Well-being of mothers and children at outset

Introduction

In this chapter we provide information about the well-being of the mothers and children of the families at the outset. This is based upon the results of the measures completed by the mothers during the first-stage face-to-face interviews. We begin by looking at the reasons for referral to the study before moving on to consider the results in detail. We report on differences between the Study and Comparison groups and any significant regional variations. Details of the measures used can be found in Chapter 1 and Appendix 2.

Referrals

All the referrals of the Comparison mothers were made by health visitors. The referrals of the Study mothers were made by health visitors and Home-Start organisers. The latter were the predominant referrers (Northern Ireland study, $n = 41$, 85.4 per cent; England study, $n = 27$, 84.4 per cent). Overall the main reasons for referral were the mothers' mental health ($n = 57$, 35.2 per cent), multiple births/multiple young children ($n = 37$, 22.8 per cent) and mothers' isolation/loneliness ($n = 34$, 21.0 per cent). These were also the predominant reasons in both the Study and Comparison groups.

There were some regional variations. With the mothers from England (Study and Comparison), the main reasons for referral were the mothers' mental health and the mothers' isolation/loneliness. With the mothers from Northern Ireland (Study and Comparison), the main reasons were multiple births, mothers' mental health and mothers' isolation/loneliness (Table 4). There was a statistically significant difference between Northern Ireland and England for the predominant reason for referral. Most of the difference could be attributed to the numbers of mothers with multiple births in Northern Ireland and England ($\chi^2 = 9.209$, d.f. $= 4$, $P = 0.050$).

Table 4 Predominant reason for referral to the study

	Mothers' mental health	Mothers' physical health	Children with special needs	Multiple births/young children	Mothers' isolation/ loneliness	Total
Study group (n)	26	6	12	22	14	80
%	32.5	7.5	15	27.5	17.5	
Comparison group (n)	31	3	13	15	20	82
%	37.8	3.7	15.9	18.3	24.4	
Total sample (n)	57	9	25	37	34	162
%	35.2	5.6	15.4	22.8	21	

Parenting stress

The majority of the mothers appeared to be experiencing a very high level of parenting stress at the time of the initial interviews. Almost two-thirds (n = 105, 64.8 per cent) of the mothers were experiencing clinically significant levels of stress (according to their scores on the Parenting Stress Index (PSI)/Total Stress score). More mothers in the Comparison than in the Study Groups were experiencing these levels (n = 55, 67.1 per cent; n = 50, 62.5 per cent, respectively). More mothers in Northern Ireland than in England were experiencing these levels (n = 61, 66.3 per cent; n = 44, 62.8 per cent, respectively). Fifty-seven per cent of all those experiencing clinically significant levels of stress were in Northern Ireland (Table 5). However, there were no statistically significant differences between the Study and Comparison groups and between the Northern Ireland and England Groups in terms of the Total Stress scores on the PSI.

Maternal mental health: postnatal depression

Almost half of the mothers (n = 76, 46.9 per cent) appeared to be suffering from a depressive illness of varying severity, scoring above the threshold of 13 on the Edinburgh Postnatal Depression Scale (EPDS) (Table 6). Almost half of the Study and Comparison mothers (n = 38, 46.3 per cent; n = 38, 47.5 per cent, respectively) also scored over the threshold (Table 7). A slightly higher percentage of mothers in Northern Ireland (n = 45, 48.9 per cent) than England (n = 31, 44.3 per cent) scored at this level. However, there were no statistically significant differences between Study and Comparison groups nor between Northern Ireland and England in terms of postnatal depression.

Maternal mental health: depression

Two-thirds of the mothers (n = 109, 67.3 per cent) appeared to have depressive symptomatology, scoring above the suggested cut-off point of 16 on the Centre for Epidemiological Studies Depression

Table 5 Parenting stress: mothers' Total Stress scores on PSI at baseline

	Clinically significant level of stress (scores >90)	High level of stress (scores >86)	Normal level of stress (scores 56–85)	Low level of stress (scores <55)
Study group (n)	50	56	23	1
% Study group	62.5	70.0	28.8	1.3
% clinically stressed mothers	49.4			
Comparison group (n)	55	59	23	0
% Comparison group	67.1	72.0	28.0	0.0
% clinically stressed mothers	50.6			
Total sample (n)	105	115	46	1
% total sample	64.8	71.0	28.4	0.6
% clinically stressed mothers	100			

Table 6 Maternal mental health (postnatal depression): mothers' mean scores on EPDS at baseline

	Mean	SD
Study group	13.85	6.07
Comparison group	13.00	6.45
Total sample	13.42	6.42

Table 7 Maternal mental health (postnatal depression): mothers' scores above and below threshold on EPDS at baseline

	Scores below the threshold ≤ 13	Scores above the threshold ≥ 14
Study group (*n*)	42	38
% Study group	52.5	47.5
Comparison group (*n*)	44	38
% Comparison group	53.7	46.3
Total sample (*n*)	86	76
% total sample	53.1	46.9

Scale (CES-D) (Table 8). This was more evident in the mothers from Northern Ireland than those from England ($n = 65$, 70.7 per cent; $n = 44$, 62.9 per cent, respectively) and slightly more evident in the Study mothers than in the Comparison mothers ($n = 57$, 71.2 per cent; $n = 52$, 63.4 per cent, respectively) (Table 9). However, there were no statistically significant differences between Study and Comparison groups nor between Northern Ireland and England groups in terms of level of depression experienced by the mothers.

Of the 118 mothers who were experiencing a high level of depression, 65 (56.8 per cent) were in Northern Ireland compared with 44 (43.2 per cent) in England. Within both areas, mothers experiencing this level of depression were fairly evenly distributed within Study and Comparison groups.

Table 8 Maternal mental health (depressive symptoms): mothers' mean scores on CES-D at baseline

	Mean	SD
Study group	25.64	13.84
Comparison group	23.06	14.38
Total sample	24.04	14.10

Table 9 Maternal mental health (depressive symptoms): mothers' low and high scores on CES-D at baseline

	Low scores (≤ 16)	High scores (16 >)
Study group (*n*)	23	57
% Study group	28.8	71.2
% of mothers with high scores		49.4
Comparison group (*n*)	30	52
% Comparison group	36.6	63.4
% of mothers with high scores		50.6
Total sample (*n*)	53	109
% total sample	32.7	67.3

Table 10 Maternal self-esteem: mothers' mean scores on RSE at baseline

	Mean	SD
Study group	25.24	5.74
Comparison group	24.85	4.71

Maternal self-esteem

The self-esteem of the mothers was measured on the Rosenberg Self-Esteem Scale (RSE), the mean score being around 25.04 (SD 5.23). No published UK norms were available to place these results in context. However, the scores served as baseline information on which we could assess progress over time. The mean scores for the Study and Comparison mothers and Northern Ireland and England mothers showed no significant differences (Table 10). However, there was a statistically significant interaction ($F_{(1, 158)} = 4.299$, $P = 0.040$) between group (Study vs. Comparison) and region (Northern Ireland vs. England). Simple effects analyses suggested that this interaction was mainly due to the relatively high mean self-esteem score of the Study group in England. While there appeared to be a marked difference between the Study and Comparison groups in England, this was not statistically significant.

Social and emotional development of selected children

Fifty-three mothers had selected one of their children, aged between 1 and 3 years, when responding to the Parenting Stress Index. These mothers were also asked to provide their views of the social and emotional adjustment of their selected child. A considerable number of mothers viewed their child's emotional and social development as problematic and/or their own competence in these areas as being deficient.

According to their scores on the Brief Infant–Toddler Social and Emotional Assessment Scale (BITSEA), 23 of the mothers perceived their child as having social–emotional or behavioural problems and 13 saw their child as having delays in the areas of competence. Nine mothers viewed their child (five boys and four girls) as having problems in both areas. The distribution is detailed in Tables 11 and 12. Overall, more mothers in Northern Ireland

Table 11 Children's social and emotional development: mothers' high problem scores on BITSEA at baseline

	Boys	Girls
Study group (*n*)	8	8
Column %	61.5	66.7
Comparison group (*n*)	3	4
Column %	38.5	33.3
Total sample (*n*)	11	12

Table 12 Children's social and emotional development: mothers' low competence scores on BITSEA at baseline

	Boys	Girls
Study group (*n*)	3	4
Column %	50.0	57.1
Comparison group (*n*)	3	3
Column %	50.0	42.9
Total sample (*n*)	6	7

Table 13 Maternal social support: mothers' mean scores on MSSI at baseline

	Mean	Median	SD
Study group	20.63	21.0	4.78
Comparison group	21.26	21.0	5.41
Total sample	20.94	21.0	5.10

Table 14 Maternal social support: mothers' scores below 15 and relative to group median on MSSI at baseline

	Scores lower than 15	Below the group median*	Group median and above
Study group (n)	7	43	37
% Study group	8.8	53.8	46.2
% mothers scoring < 15	46.6		
Comparison group (n)	8	42	40
% Comparison group	9.8	51.2	48.8
% mothers scoring < 15	53.3		
Total sample (n)	15	85	67
% total sample	9.2	52.5	47.5
% mothers scoring < 15	100		

* This includes scores below 15 in all groups.

(35.5 per cent) than England (9.5 per cent) saw their child as having delays in competence. This difference was found to be significant ($\chi^2 = 4.50$, d.f. = 1, $P = 0.034$).

Maternal social support

More than half of the mothers ($n = 85$, 52.5 per cent) assessed the level of emotional and tangible support available to them to be at a relatively low level. On the Maternal Social Support Index (MSSI) similar proportions of the Study and Comparison mothers scored below the median score for their respective group ($n = 43$, 53.8 per cent; $n = 42$, 51.2 per cent, respectively). Fifteen mothers scored lower than 15, indicating difficult and isolated lives. Eight of the 15 mothers who were experiencing difficult, isolated lives were in the Comparison group, in contrast to seven in the Study group (Tables 13 and 14). There were no statistically significant differences between the Study and Comparison groups nor between the

Northern Ireland and England groups in terms of maternal social support.

Summary

Results of the outcome measures at baseline corresponded closely with the information provided by the mothers at interview. These mothers were experiencing a very high level of parenting stress at the time of the initial interviews. Some of the mothers had concerns about the social and emotional development of their children. Almost half of the mothers appeared to be suffering from a postnatal depressive illness, while two-thirds appeared to have more general depressive symptomatology, suggesting widespread problems, often of a severe nature.

Given the level and extent of stress expressed by these mothers and their mental health difficulties, it was of particular concern that many of the mothers seemed to have a relatively low level of emotional and tangible support available to them.

5 Mothers' perspectives at follow-up

Introduction

In this chapter we present the views of the mothers at the time of the follow-up interviews. All the mothers were asked about the stresses they were experiencing at the outset, whether they were still present and to what extent. In the initial section on parenting stress, we present the broad patterns based upon the responses of the entire sample of 162 mothers. Following that, we return to the 42 mothers who had the average number of stress factors at the initial interview to gain an in-depth understanding of the changes over time. Finally, all of the Study mothers were also asked about the support they had received from Home-Start. Follow-up case studies of the families described in Chapter 3 are included for illustration.

Parenting stress

At the follow-up interviews, all of the mothers (162) were asked if they were still experiencing the stresses previously identified and, if so, to what extent. In the analysis, we focused upon those mothers who had experienced the five most frequently mentioned stress factors (maternal mental health; lack of support; multiple demands; financial; parenting issues) and explored the nature and extent of change, if any (Table 15).

The majority of both Study and Comparison mothers indicated that there was improvement in these areas of stress, or there was no longer any stress associated with them. The one exception to this was in the area of stresses associated with finance.

Almost three-quarters of the Study and Comparison mothers with mental health problems reported improvement, and approximately two-thirds of both groups who had experienced a lack of support indicated an improvement. There were some differences between the two groups. A higher percentage of the Study mothers who had been experiencing stresses related to multiple demands or financial issues reported improvement. The reverse was true for stresses related to parenting issues and child behaviour. Generally, over this period both groups of mothers appeared to experience least improvement in stresses related to financial matters.

Emergent themes from the mothers' interviews

As with the first-stage interviews, we focused again on the 42 families (drawn from the Study and Comparison groups) who were experiencing the average number (six) of stresses. The emergent themes that arose from this analysis are detailed below.

Pregnancy/birth trauma and mothers' well-being postbirth

Returning to the mothers approximately a year later, it was obvious that many of the initial health

Table 15 Most frequently cited stress factors: nature and extent of change at follow up [Study (S) and Comparison (C) groups]

Stress	No longer present		To lesser extent		To same extent		To greater extent	
	S	C	S	C	S	C	S	C
Mothers' mental health	25	16	20	31	14	9	4	9
Multiple demands	12	13	35	15	8	7	9	7
Financial	9	6	11	11	13	13	6	8
Lack of support	22	30	29	11	18	14	8	8
Parenting issues / children's behaviour	8	13	9	14	11	5	4	5

problems experienced by the mothers and their babies were no longer present. Early issues with feeding and reflux problems appeared to have been largely resolved. At times these were resolved through normal development of the babies and at others through professional or medical advice/intervention.

Transition to parenthood

On the whole, at the follow-up interviews, most of the mothers were experiencing less stress. Generally, the babies had well-established sleeping patterns and in turn their mothers were experiencing a full night's sleep. Perhaps the most remarkable difference with these mothers was their increased sense of confidence both in themselves and as mothers. Very often this appeared to have developed as a result of having faced their worst fears, i.e. their children taking ill and needing hospitalisation, and finding that they could cope in these situations. Interestingly, there did not appear to be any one factor associated with the rise in their confidence. Rather, it seemed that over time they had begun to build up their confidence through their own resolve. Of course, not all of the mothers had increased their confidence to a much higher level. However, quite a number of the others were showing signs of taking steps towards increasing their social networks and friendships. There was also a strong sense of most of these mothers having adjusted to the situation they found themselves in and accepting that they could not immediately change it. As a result of this shift of attitude, many mothers described themselves as feeling much calmer in themselves and as parents. Many of the mothers conveyed a new positive attitude to their lives in general and parenting in particular. They described establishing routines with their children and in their household management, ensuring time for themselves and setting aside time to pursue their own development and social life. Overall, there was a sense of these women having resumed control over their lives. In many cases, the mothers' increased sense of confidence and of

regaining control over their lives was associated with a return to employment. This resulted in increased social contact, additional finance to the household and, more often than not, a sense of more equitable sharing of the responsibility of parenting with their partners.

I think probably I can cope with it better … Whenever you have a new baby, it's so much harder anyway.

I'm not so worried about housework and stuff now because I think there's more important things with the children.

I'm going out for a meal with some friends and he [partner] is baby-sitting, so he'll just have to get on with it.

Multiple demands of young children on one adult

Many of the mothers appeared to be finding the multiple demands of young dependent children much less stressful than a year previously. In many cases this was a result of additional support/respite for the mothers. Sometimes it seemed to be due to the fact that the children were at different developmental stages a year later and the younger children were less dependent on adult help. At times it was due to the mothers and their partners having reached a better level of communication and more equitable sharing of responsibilities in caring for the children. Perhaps more remarkably was the mothers who did not appear to have more support but who were approaching the matter with a significantly different attitude. They were actively seeking means of regular respite. Generally, such respite came through the use of playgroups, nurseries, crèches or when the children entered primary school. Very often these mothers appeared to have developed new approaches to coping with the multiple demands being placed upon them. They had found resolutions that worked for them and were much less concerned about the opinion of others as to how they reached such resolutions.

I think it's a combination of both ... With me going back to work, you have to get into a routine. And now that he's older ... he can take his own bottle now and ... sit up and watch TV.

Lack of available support and need for respite

Generally, fewer mothers appeared to be experiencing isolation or a lack of support at follow-up interviews. At times this was due to a resolution of estranged relations with wider families or move of accommodation to be nearer family members who would provide support. Sometimes it was the availability of a car that allowed them to travel and at least be in the company of families even if the families could not provide actual respite. There were a number of situations where the husbands' work hours or job changed, facilitating sharing responsibilities of the children and more time together as couples. Two of the Study families particularly mentioned that their Home-Start volunteer had been a valuable support in encouraging them to get out of the house and to make new friendships. Sometimes, as a result of support from friends or their volunteers or simply as a result of their children being older and now attending playgroups, some of the mothers were in positions where they had the opportunity to make friends easily with other mothers of young children in the area. Again, it was very evident that many mothers were setting about changing this aspect of their lives to take a more positive direction , taking active steps to address it.

I've just got friendly with a lot more mums at school and ... even though I only see them at the beginning of school and at the end of school ... it's still that little bit of adult contact that ... sometimes was lacking. And so I feel ... that's really improved.

The car means I can get out ... with G [eldest child] being at playgroup... I see other mothers so you can chat ... at least I'm getting out and seeing other people with having transport.

Mothers' mental health

The vast majority of both the Study and Comparison group mothers indicated positive changes in their mental health or an absence of the problem altogether at the time of follow-up. This was in line with the findings from the overall sample discussed earlier.

The mothers attributed positive change in their mental health to a variety of factors, both personal and associated with their social networks/ supports. Several also indicated that anti-depressants had helped. Perhaps the most outstanding feature was the number of mothers who appeared to have adopted a more positive attitude and had become increasingly confident in themselves and as parents. Other parents clearly attributed the change to the availability of respite facilities. Some of the Study mothers clearly thought the reason for the change was the support they had received from Home-Start. Others related it to returning to work, or simply a gradual adjustment to parenthood. A couple of mothers stated that support from their families had made the difference. Other factors given included improved physical health of the mothers and the mothers' gradual acceptance of their current life situation. A couple of the mothers also indicated that the fact that their children were older, and at a different developmental stage that meant they were less dependent on them, had made a substantial difference. (Although this was only mentioned by a couple of mothers in this selected group, it was a recurrent feature of the responses of the mothers in the overall sample.) Other factors stated by the mothers included improvement in the children's behaviour, improvement in financial situations and an increased sense of joy in their children and the children's development.

Because the depression has gone, I feel that I can cope with anything ... There's been no suicidal thoughts in a long time. The medication I would think too has helped.

I do go out quite a lot now ... I've got my confidence back. That's probably due to W, my best friend ... When I lost touch with these people [friends] I felt cut-off but now they've all come back again ... my old friends ... my old life ... so I think that's helped a lot.

I think maybe getting back out and ... going back to work and sort of getting part of my old life back again ... getting back into work again, you know getting back into normality or back into ... the way things were before you had the baby.

Several of the mothers had indicated that they now had the opportunity for regular respite from full-time care of their young children and thought that this had made a significant difference to their mental health. This respite was being provided by wider family members or through the use of playgroups. While only one mother particularly mentioned the use of a playgroup here, the value of playgroups and nurseries for respite was referred to by many mothers in the overall sample.

Probably people around helping me and knowing that they were there you know if I need them.

Three of the Study mothers attributed in their improved mental health directly to the support they had received from Home-Start.

I've had B [Home-Start volunteer]. She has been coming once a week and she is a brilliant help. She can talk to you as a friend and even just ... help with the children. She would come and read them a story ... if I do something around the house ... She's a good help to me.

Parenting a child/children with special needs and/or behavioural problems

Many of the mothers reported that there had been significant changes in the stresses they were experiencing associated with caring for children with special needs. This was reportedly due to placement in nurseries, assessment of learning needs by educational psychologists, placement in special schools or nurseries, the provision of speech therapy or private tutoring.

However, a significant number of parents were reporting the same level of stress or higher at the follow-up interviews. These mothers were reporting ongoing difficulties with their children's behaviour or indeed an increase in problematic behaviour with an increase in the age of the children. In a few cases, the mothers were still seeking a diagnosis of their children's condition/special needs, and were extremely concerned about this. Several mothers expressed disappointment or anger about the lack of services to support families of children with special needs.

Mothers' physical health/disability

On the whole the physical health problems that appeared to be related to pregnancy, birth or postbirth complications appeared to have been resolved by the time of follow-up interviews. Several of the mothers who had been anticipating hospitalisation as a result of their own health issues had had successful treatment. Others with long-term health problems, such as thyroid difficulties or arthritis, were experiencing the same level as at the earlier interview. One mother who was registered blind was experiencing a higher level of stress as her child was now older and hence more active and difficult to supervise.

Financial worries

Of all of the areas of stress identified by the mothers, financial worries was the area showing least change by the time of the follow-up interviews. Many of the mothers had returned to work during the period between the two interviews. This did seem to mean that these families were in a better financial position and more able to meet the needs of the growing children. However, other mothers, particularly those who were caring for children on their own, appeared to be still very concerned about their financial situations. A few reported that they were in considerable debt. Many of the mothers in the overall sample, as well as this subsample, reported that they were simply existing from week to week on the bare necessities.

> *We're just about managing month by month ... but if anything happens ... needs doing or whatever ... we haven't got the money to do it. We just don't feel like we're actually progressing towards anything and you know all the time the girls get older, they start requiring more and more things.*

Mothers' relationship with ex-husbands/ex-partners

On the whole there appeared to be considerable improvement in this area for most mothers. The improvement seemed to be related to divorce court hearings having been held during the year and resolutions over access having been reached. Sometimes there was simply no further contact with the ex-partner and consequently a reduction in conflict. In some cases there was evidence of ex-partners taking greater responsibility for the care of their children through regular weekend care.

> *The fact that he's [ex-partner] in contact more ... their moods ... I had to deal with that and I don't have to deal with that because he's in regular contact now.*

> *He [ex-partner] is more willing to have the children ... Although it is only from a Saturday to the Sunday evening (each fortnight) still, you know you're going to get a break at some time.*

Home-Start support and expectations

Mothers' general reactions

All of the Study mothers were asked about the support they had received from Home-Start and the extent to which it met their expectations. The vast majority of mothers reported that they had received one visit of approximately 2 hours per week. Approximately a quarter of the mothers also reported that they had telephone contact with their volunteers between visits, or had been given their telephone numbers to use should they wish to do so.

The volunteers offered a range of practical and/or emotional support. This included listening to the mothers, accompanying them and the children out to the shops or to mother and toddler groups, or simply providing respite to the mothers by taking the children out to local parks or minding them in their own home. During these brief periods the mothers were generally carrying out household chores and necessary errands, spending time with their children or simply catching up with much needed sleep.

> *She has been very good. She's been there for me from when I lost N [baby]. She's still there now and if I am upset she'll talk to me on the 'phone and calm me down. She also gives me a break if I am tired and stressed and she plays with L [child] the whole time she's here to give me a rest. Yeah she's very good, I get letters that I can't understand and she will go through them.*

> *The children have always known that on those 3 days we would be making things. We would be going to the park. Or I'd sit and I'd do sticking with them or painting or something like that. And they used to get excited when they saw her car coming down the road because they knew that we were going to do something nice.*

A number of the mothers also described the benefits of being able to talk to someone unknown and appreciated the fact that their volunteers offered a non-judgmental listening ear.

> *I could talk to her, which was a big weight off my shoulders, which just helped me so much and she didn't judge or anything, which was the best thing.*

Many of the mothers described how they valued the support of and contact with their Home-Start volunteers. Many indicated that the relationship between themselves and the volunteers had developed into a friendship.

It's having someone there really that is like a mum to me really ... and a mum and a best friend. You know she has always been there and even if it is not her day to visit and she rings and I'm really down she will make time out to come round and help.

Parenting stress and the impact of Home-Start

All of the mothers were asked if they thought that the Home-Start support had made a difference in relation to the stresses they were experiencing at the time of the first interview. More than four-fifths (65) of the mothers indicated that they thought it had. They tended to portray Home-Start support as providing a general sense of relief from overwhelming pressure.

Some of the mothers described how Home-Start had helped to alleviate their sense of isolation. Furthermore, a significant number indicated that receiving support from Home-Start had helped to increase their self-confidence.

Well I think mainly ... just talking and sharing cups of tea and listening. Being human. I didn't have anyone else to be human with, you know what I mean. I didn't have a friend particularly who could come at that time and just be willing to do that.

It was actually J [volunteer] that persuaded me to get driving lessons and learn how to drive and ... It definitely made me more confident.

Some of the women highlighted that the Home-Start support also helped to improve their mental health.

Because then I had nobody to talk to ... I was bottling my feelings up ... J [volunteer]: she's a really nice girl. She would have talked about anything ... It helped me with ... the stress of ... having the depression.

The majority of mothers welcomed the opportunity simply to be able to talk to someone, and some found it valuable for ventilating deeply felt emotions. They found that the volunteers were able to relate to their situation.

You know, seeing P [volunteer] for that short time every week was an opening for releasing some of the frustration and the anger and the hurt and ... everything.

Some of the mothers thought that Home-Start had had a positive impact on their children. They reported a general enhancement in the well-being of their children, an increase in their social activities, or an improvement in the mother–child relationships.

H [volunteer] always brought her wee girl with her so ... she [daughter] was mixing with another child ... She loved getting out in the car.

She gave D [child] lots of confidence ... She would ask D about his day at school and what he'd been doing, and about his friends. And he felt that he was being treated like a grown-up. So, that in turn gave him confidence in the fact that things he was doing were important and that somebody was interested.

Additionally, a number of the mothers also described how Home-Start provided benefits to their partners and / or had a positive influence on their relationships.

It meant that he hasn't got the shopping to do in the evening.

I think it made a big difference ... It took the pressure off him because he wasn't the sole kind of emotional support for me.

I think he found it easier 'cause one of the problems was that he was finding it very hard to actually leave the house because he knew that sometimes I was very unhappy ... if he knew that I had something during the day that I was looking forward to then that made it easier for him.

Expectations and outcomes

All of the mothers were asked to what extent their expectations of Home-Start matched the outcomes. The majority of mothers ($n = 60$, 75 per cent) reported that the support they received from

Home-Start either met their expectations or in some cases exceeded them.

> I think I've got more than I expected out of it because I have been pleasantly surprised at the family outings... I've enjoyed that.

> All I wanted was that wee break ... as much as I love my child ... I just needed a break for a couple of hours in the week ... just for 'me' time ... that's what I wanted out of it and that is what I got out of it, you know, which was good.

> It was brilliant, it really was ... As I say, I spent more time with the child where normally you would have the children here running about ... I would give it 10 out of 10.

In contrast, 12 (15 per cent) of the mothers reported that Home-Start failed to match their expectations. Generally their disappointment was based upon the service, in their view, not assisting with respite, being offered too late or failing to help them reduce their isolation or simply not appearing to be interested in helping them. A small number thought that their volunteers appeared not to be interested in helping them.

> It is no good her coming to sit here ... I need her [volunteer] to take the children out.

> When they [twins] were first born, that's when I really needed help ... I didn't get them [Home-Start] until they were 4 months old ...

> I thought that ... she [volunteer] would be calling ... to help me. She'd call in and I would say, 'Do you want a cup of tea?' and then she would have a cigarette and then she would go ... If I had ... been somebody who was really depending on her calling, I would have been lost.

Amount of support offered by Home-Start

A significant number of mothers indicated that while they thought that Home-Start was a helpful support, a weekly short visit was not sufficient to make a significant difference to their everyday stresses.

> I think practically it is a great idea. The two hours were great but to make a difference, it needs to be a bit more intense.

> It's not really much ... 2 hours wasn't much, really, at the end of the day ... I don't think it was long enough really ... Two hours a week wouldn't do much to relieve the stress.

Other support received by the mothers between first and second interviews

Most mothers (Study and Comparison) indicated that they had turned to families, friends and professionals for occasional support. There was very little evidence of other formal family support services being offered or received in the intervening period.

Case Study: Study family B at follow-up

At the follow-up interview the mother reported that some of the original stresses were still present, while others were not. Her mental health had improved. She no longer had the postnatal depression and had not suffered any panic attacks in the previous 6 months. She continued to see a psychiatrist once every 3 months, while the community psychiatric nurse visited every few weeks. She had spent approximately 6 weeks in a psychiatric hospital within the previous year. However, she was no longer experiencing suicidal thoughts. She was still on medication. Nevertheless, she helped set up a support group for women with postnatal depression in the area.

She was still concerned about her son, who was still displaying behaviour problems but to a lesser extent. She realised that she was more patient with him now and attributed this to changes in her own mental health. She was no longer feeling as isolated because she

(Continued)

had returned to part-time employment, and this had also eased the financial situation. Participating in the postnatal depression group had also helped.

Home-Start provided mainly emotional support and friendship to this mother. Her Home-Start volunteer had been visiting for 2 hours every week for 8 months. They would go into the town or meet for lunch or the mother would go up to the volunteer's house. The volunteer also provided the mother with information on after-school groups, crèches and other types of support available to her. This mother thought that the Home-Start support had reduced her sense of isolation, provided her with someone to talk to, enhanced her self-esteem and encouraged her to have interests outside of her home.

Case study: Comparison family C at follow-up

At the follow-up interview this mother indicated that some of the original stresses were still present whilst others were not. She was no longer experiencing sleep problems. Having moved house she was no longer constantly reminded about the assault.

One of this mother's major concerns at the initial interview was finance. She remained worried about this at second interview, commenting that more costs seemed to be incurred as the children grew older. She was still coping alone with the multiple demands of four children. However, she was less isolated now as she had made significant changes in her life. In her own words, 'I've changed my life completely and I've got new friends and I've got access to a car'.

(Continued)

Additionally, her child was no longer a concern as he appeared to have made significant progress over time. She remarked, 'I think he's just grew up a lot … Even in nursery, the teacher said … he's like a different child'. This mother indicated that she had developed a whole new outlook on life. Moreover, she thought that participating in the initial research interview had given her the opportunity to reflect on her situation. This, in turn, had made her decide to change things for the better.

This mother indicated that she would still welcome more people to turn to for support. For instance, someone to provide respite or someone to play with the children. She had asked on several occasions for a family support worker. However, at the time of the second interview she was still waiting for one.

Summary

The general picture at the follow-up stage was of a much improved situation for most mothers. Almost three-quarters of the maternal mental health problems had improved or were no longer present. Two-thirds of the mothers were also reporting an improvement in the support available to them. The one area where there was least improvement was finance.

We looked again at the 42 mothers who had the average number of stresses at the initial interview to get a more in-depth understanding of what had brought about the changes or indeed lack of change over time. Most of the issues surrounding the transition to parenthood were resolved. There was much evidence of the mothers having increased confidence as parents, largely through experience. Overall they appeared to have resumed control over their lives. An important change was that the children were older and less dependent. There was evidence of an increase in their social networks, often through return to work, an increase in finance and at times a more equitable sharing of parenting responsibilities with their partners/husbands. With regard to multiple demands and the associated stress, these appeared to be much less evident, often as a result of additional support/respite. Even where mothers did not have any more support than before, they had changed their attitude. They were proactive in seeking respite and appeared more generally to have a new approach to coping with demands.

Nevertheless, some mothers of children with special needs reported that there was no change or that the level of stress was worse. These mothers reported that as the children grew older their problems increased. Often they had been waiting for diagnosis of complex special needs for lengthy periods or they were disappointed about the lack of services available. Also, for those mothers with chronic long-term health conditions, there was no improvement. For these mothers, the increasing age of the children and the consequent rise in activity added to their levels of stress. In general, the area of finance showed least improvement. In particular, lone mothers often remained worried about their financial situation and several reported that they were in considerable debt.

Home-Start support to the Study mothers generally consisted of a weekly visit by the volunteer to the mothers' homes for approximately 2 hours per week. The volunteers offered a range of practical and emotional support. Most mothers thought that the support had made a difference. Reasons offered included alleviating their sense of isolation, increasing their self-confidence and improving their mental health, as well as having a positive impact on the quality of their children's lives. For the most part, having the support of a Home-Start volunteer seemed to provide a general sense of relief from overwhelming pressure. However, a significant number of the mothers indicated that, while they thought that Home-Start was a helpful support, the intensity of service was insufficient to make a substantial difference to their everyday stresses.

With regard to other support received by both groups in the intervening period between both interviews, most mothers in both groups indicated that they had received occasional informal support from families and/or friends. They had also consulted a range of professionals. There was virtually no evidence of support from any other form of family support service being received by these families.

6 Well-being of mothers and children over time

Introduction

This chapter examines the well-being of the mothers and children of the families over time. This is based on the results of the measures completed by the mothers at both first- and second-stage interviews. The results, apart from those relating to the BITSEA, are based on the full sample of 80 Study mothers and 82 Comparison mothers who completed the measures at baseline and follow-up interviews. As in Chapter 4, we report on any differences between the mothers in the Study (Home-Start) group and those in the Comparison group and any significant regional variations.

Parenting stress

In general, the mothers were experiencing less parenting stress at follow-up. Also there was evidence of a decrease in the numbers of mothers who were experiencing the highest level of stress. At the time of the first interviews, there were significantly more mothers experiencing stress at a clinically significant level than not in both the Study and Comparison groups. Fortunately, at follow-up, this was no longer the case for either group.

However, there was no significant difference in the reduction in parenting stress over time between the Study group mothers (who had received Home-Start support) and the Comparison group mothers, according to the results on the Parenting Stress Index (PSI)/Total Stress score (Table 16 and Figure 4).

Table 16 Parenting stress: mothers' mean scores on PSI at baseline and follow-up

	Baseline measure (stage 1) Mean (SD)	Follow-up measure (stage 2) Mean (SD)
Study group	97.975 (20.335)	88.125 (20.161)
Comparison group*	100.543 (21.344)	88.926 (20.138)

* Due to one incomplete response on this scale, only 81 Comparison mothers were included in the analysis.

Figure 4 Parenting stress: mothers' mean PSI Total Stress scores across groups and over time

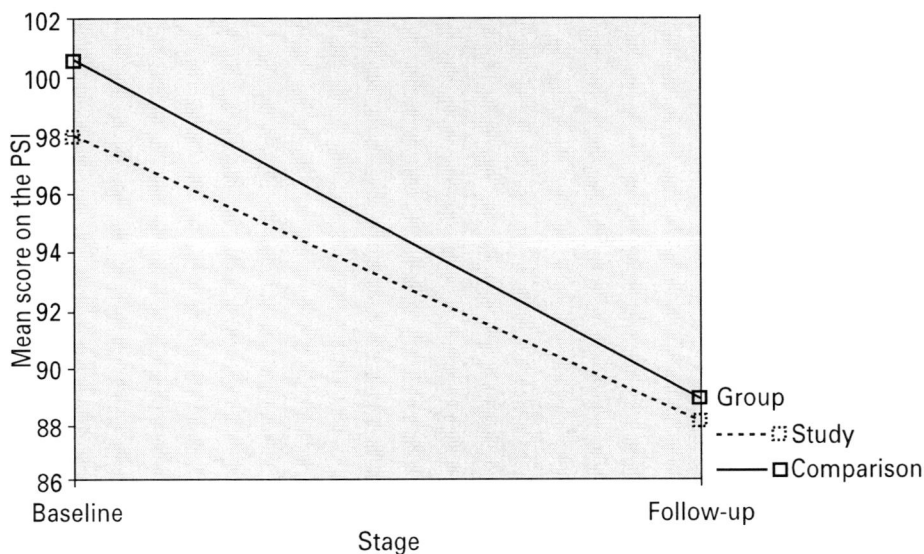

Maternal mental health: postnatal depression and depression

Overall, there was a general decrease in the level of depression experienced by mothers in both the Study and Comparison groups over time. The level of depression, according to the results of both the Edinburgh Postnatal Depression Scale (EPDS) and the Centre for Epidemiological Studies Depression Scale (CES-D), decreased at a similar rate for both groups (Study and Comparison) over time (Tables 17 and 18 and Figures 5 and 6).

Regarding the EPDS, as indicated in Chapter 1, those who scored at or above a threshold score of 13 were considered to be suffering from a depressive illness of varying severity. The overall mean scores for both the Study and Comparison group mothers at the time of the first interviews suggested that these mothers were suffering depression at that point. At follow-up, the scores were lower for both sets of mothers, suggesting that there was improvement in this area for both groups. However, there was no significant difference in the level of improvement between the two groups. The same trend was evident with the CES-D results.

Table 17 Maternal mental health (postnatal depression): mothers' mean scores on EPDS at baseline and follow-up

	Baseline measure (stage 1) Mean (SD)	Follow-up measure (stage 2) Mean (SD)
Study group	13.850 (6.072)	10.050 (5.585)
Comparison group	13.000 (6.745)	9.963 (6.147)

Figure 5 Maternal mental health (postnatal depression): mothers' mean scores on EPDS across groups and over time

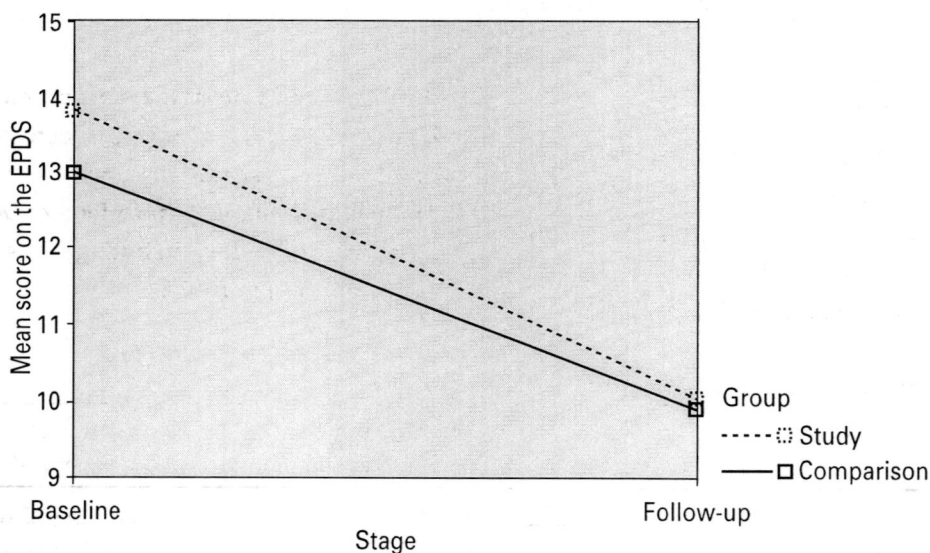

Table 18 Maternal mental health (depressive symptoms): mothers' mean scores on CES-D at baseline and follow-up

	Baseline measure (stage 1) Mean (SD)	Follow-up measure (stage 2) Mean (SD)
Study group	25.038 (13.836)	16.938 (13.281)
Comparison group	23.061 (14.377)	16.938 (13.468)

Figure 6 Maternal mental health (depressive symptoms): mothers' mean scores on CES-D across groups and over time

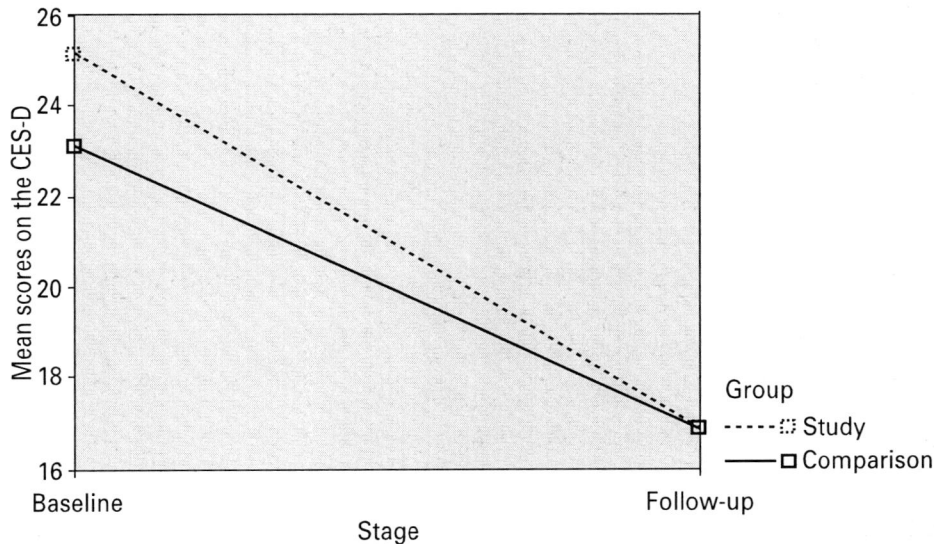

Maternal self-esteem

Overall, the self-esteem of the mothers increased over time. Results of the Rosenberg Self-Esteem Scale (RSE) indicated an increase in the level of self-esteem of the mothers in both the Study and Comparison groups over time. The self-esteem of the Study and Comparison group mothers increased at a similar rate. (A decrease in the score of this scale indicates an increase in self-esteem.) There was no significant difference between the scores of the mothers in both groups at follow-up (Table 19 and Figure 7).

Table 19 Maternal self-esteem: mothers' mean scores on RSE at baseline and follow-up

	Baseline measure (stage 1) Mean (SD)	Follow-up measure (stage 2) Mean (SD)
Study group	25.238 (5.744)	22.025 (5.548)
Comparison group	24.854 (4.709)	22.658 (6.000)

Figure 7 Maternal self-esteem: mothers' mean scores on RSE across groups and over time

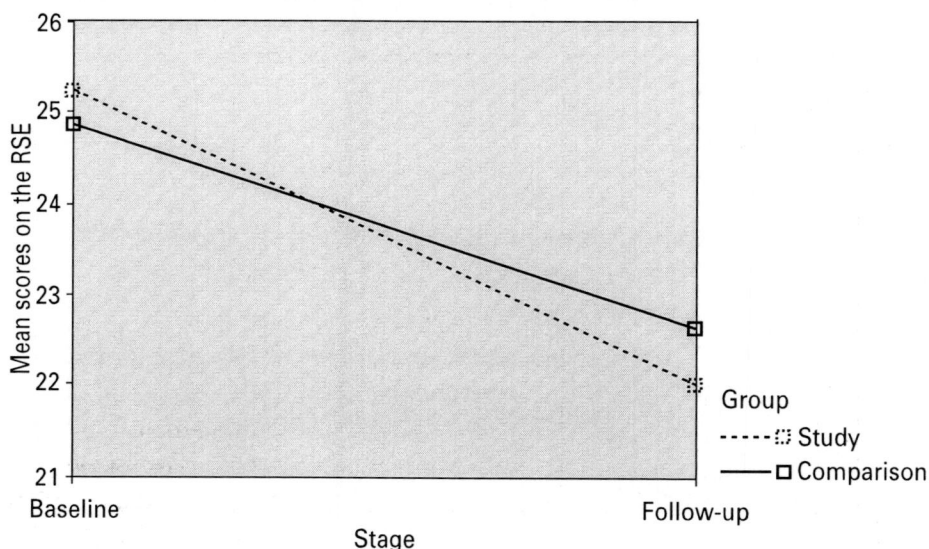

Social and emotional development of selected children

Of the 53 mothers who initially participated, 49 responded at both stages. Hence our analysis of change over time was based only on these informants. Overall, there was an improvement over time in the social and emotional development of the children, according to the mothers' ratings on the Brief Infant–Toddler Social and Emotional Assessment Scale (BITSEA). Both groups improved at a similar rate on both the problem and competence subscales. There were no significant differences between the two groups over time (Tables 20 and 21 and Figures 8 and 9).

Table 20 Children's social and emotional development: mothers' mean scores on BITSEA (problem subscale) at baseline and follow-up

	Baseline measure (stage 1) Mean (SD)	Follow-up measure (stage 2) Mean (SD)	No. of respondents
Study group	14.700 (7.106)	10.967 (8.002)	30
Comparison group	13.474 (9.896)	12.579 (10.453)	19

Table 21 Children's social and emotional development: mothers' mean scores on BITSEA (competence subscale) at baseline and follow-up

	Baseline measure (stage 1) Mean (SD)	Follow-up measure (stage 2) Mean (SD)	No. of respondents
Study group	16.167 (3.174)	16.633 (3.388)	30
Comparison group	15.000 (3.464)	16.526 (3.389)	19

Figure 8 Children's social and emotional development: mothers' mean scores on BITSEA (problem subscale) across groups and over time

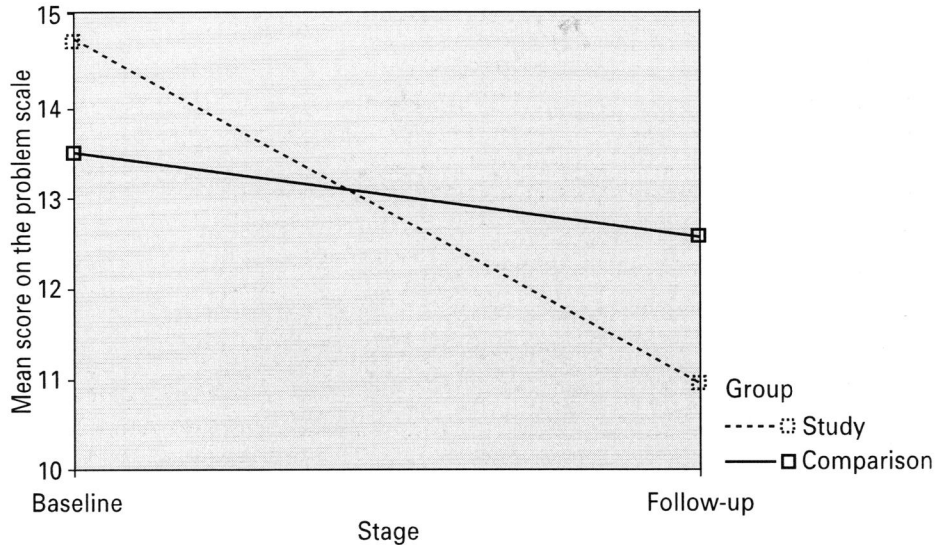

Figure 9 Children's social and emotional development: mothers' mean scores on BITSEA (competence subscale) across groups and over time

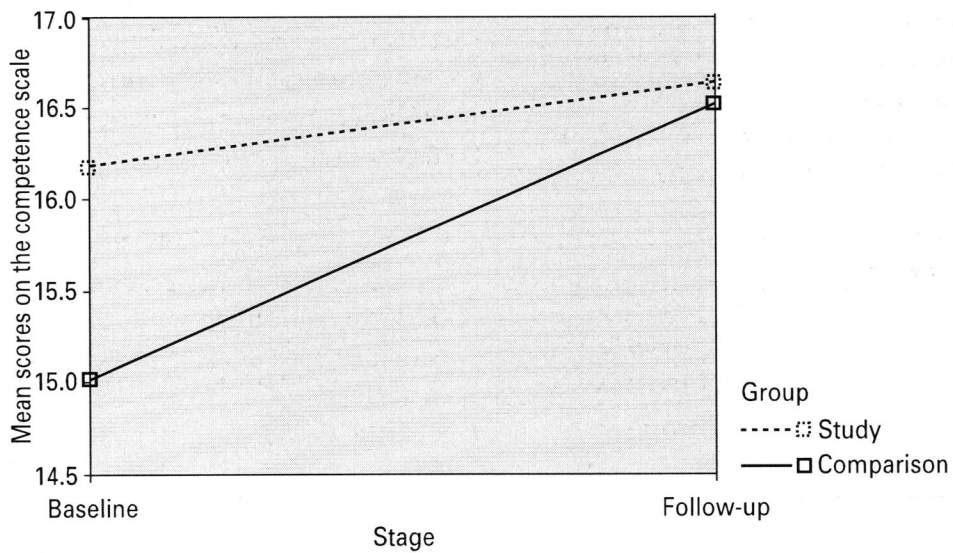

Table 22 Maternal social support: mothers' mean scores on MSSI at baseline and follow-up

	Baseline measure (stage 1) Mean (SD)	Follow-up measure (stage 2) Mean (SD)
Study group	20.625 (4.782)	22.325 (5.591))
Comparison group	21.256 (5.411)	23.101 (5.602)

Figure 10 Maternal social support: mothers' mean scores on MSSI across groups and over time

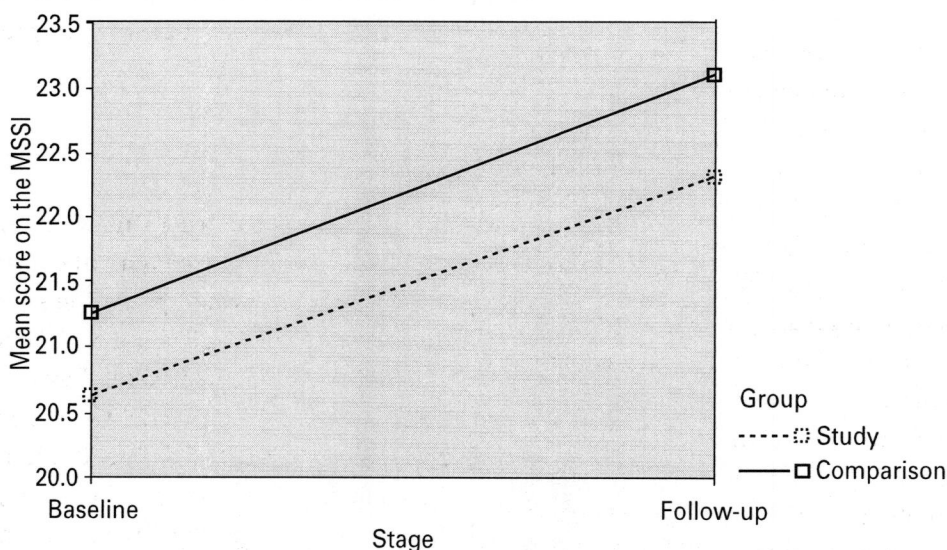

Maternal social support

Overall, at follow-up the mothers appeared to have more support. For both the Study and Comparison group mothers, scores on the Maternal Social Support Index (MSSI) increased over time. However, the increase was approximately the same for both groups and there was no significant difference between the scores of the mothers in both groups (Table 22 and Figure 10).

Home-Start support provided to families

It was important to understand how Home-Start volunteers supported the families. For this reason, we asked the volunteers to complete a form designed in collaboration with the Home-Start organisers, the Volunteer Activity Form (VAF). Information was collected on the type, frequency and duration of support offered to the families by the volunteers. They were asked to complete this form at the end of the first, sixth and twelfth (or final) month of contact with the family.

Type, frequency and duration of support
The most frequently recorded type of support was emotional, followed by practical assistance and finally help with outings. The families were visited generally three to four times per month and each visit lasted an average of approximately 2.25 to 2.50 hours.

Over time Home-Start volunteers provided significantly more emotional help, rather than practical help or help with outings, to the mothers in the study. The amount of practical support remained fairly constant throughout the course of the study. However, the amount of help with outings increased significantly and the amount of emotional help decreased over the course of the study.

Volunteers also reported a significant decrease over time in the number of visits per month and consequently time spent with the families, as the average length of each visit did not change over time.

Telephone calls were made to and received from the families and sometimes made on behalf of the families during the first month of contact. However, this did not appear to be the general pattern after this period.

When we examined the relationship between what support was offered by Home-Start and changes in the families over time, we found that the amount of practical or emotional support or help with outings was not significantly related to change on any outcome measure. However, there was little variation within the sample. This would not rule out the possibility that greater variation in the content and frequency of the service might result in different outcomes.

The average length of time that the mothers received Home-Start support was 9 months. The length of time mothers had been receiving Home-Start was not related to changes on the outcome measures. Similarly, there was no significant relationship between scores on the outcome measures and the length of time between interviews.

Receipt of other services

An important consideration to set alongside the findings presented in this chapter was any quantitative information available on whether the two groups of mothers might have been in receipt of other services that may have contributed to the results. As a result we carried out some further analysis on information gathered on services through the Client Service Receipt Inventory (CSRI) (Beecham and Knapp, 2001).

We found that the mothers in both the Study and Comparison groups received similar levels of other services at first and second interviews. Some differences were found but the inclusion of services received did not alter any of the results reported above.

Demographic variable and baseline outcome results

Finally, further analyses were carried out to investigate the influence of demographic variables, such as child age and gender and household composition, on the baseline outcome scores. It was found that no demographic variable changed the pattern of differences between the groups as described.

Summary

In general, this was a positive picture, with the mothers showing improvement over time regarding their level of parenting stress, depression and self-esteem. The level of social support available to them appeared to have increased. There was also improvement in the emotional and social development of their children between the first and second interviews. However, the overall finding was that mothers who received Home-Start and those who did not appeared to show similar levels of improvement on all of these areas.

We then turned to examine the influence of Home-Start content on the results but found no relationship between the type or duration of support and changes on the outcome measures. We explored the possibility that receipt of other services might have influenced the results. However, we found that the mothers in both the Study and Comparison groups received similar levels of other services at first and second interviews. Some differences were found but the inclusion of services received did not alter any of the results. Finally we returned to the first-stage results to examine the influence of demographic variables on the first-stage outcome scores. However, none of the demographic variables changed the pattern of differences between the two groups. In the final chapter these results are discussed in further detail.

7 Services, supports and costs over time

Introduction

Previous chapters have described important changes in the circumstances, needs and stresses experienced by families. Here we turn to the services that supported families during the study period and their associated costs. In describing the economic circumstances, service-use patterns and costs, we compare two periods of 3 months, one immediately prior to the baseline interview and the other immediately preceding the follow-up interview.

The experiences of three families help to illustrate the mix of services and supports that were used (case studies D, E and F).

Case study D

This family, mother, toddler and new baby, was referred because of the mother's mental health problems. Although the children's grandmother and friends had been very supportive the mother was depressed and very anxious about coping with difficulties alone. The children's father remained in contact but this was very stressful. The mother did not take any medication but found postnatal depression counselling helpful and had seen a psychiatrist twice. She had regular contact with a health visitor, again a helpful relationship, and saw a GP for children's check-ups and to discuss her health problems. The toddler went to playgroup once a week.

The children's father provided some financial support but the mother hoped to return to work after maternity leave. She had sought advice from a voluntary organisation about her financial worries. The mother would have liked someone to talk to and someone who would look after the toddler while she did the housework.

(Continued)

At the follow-up interview, the family was living in the same house and the mother had returned to work. She was feeling a lot better about things generally. She was getting a divorce from the children's father but both children had stayed with him for a couple of nights. The mother had a new partner who was also employed full-time. Friends and family provided support and the grandmother looked after both children during the week, taking the toddler to playgroup for four mornings. The younger child had 'glue ear' and saw the GP and had his hearing tested. The mother had a health check.

Case study E

In this family there were four children under 10, including a new baby. The mother usually worked part-time although was on maternity leave at the time of the first interview. The father had recently taken 5 weeks off work for an operation but had been able to help around the home. The mother really appreciated this as she found it 'difficult to fit everything in with the new baby'. Having four children meant 'it's just running backwards and forwards ...' to get the children to their schools and after-school activities. A health visitor did the usual baby checks and provided valuable emotional support. The eldest child saw a GP and the mother had seen a solicitor over an accident at school.

The family had moved into the area quite recently and now had little support from their relatives. The mother had made a couple of friends who would provide child care on a reciprocal basis. She would have appreciated 'an extra pair of hands, someone to talk to',

(Continued)

particularly just after the baby was born. Usually the mother felt she coped on her own, occasionally feeling tired and weepy but not depressed.

By the follow-up interview, the family had moved into a larger house and mother had given up work. She was thinking about leaving the children's father. The children were still involved in a range of activities but again few formal services were used. The father had seen a chiropractor; the local A&E department and outpatient clinics were used for common childhood ailments, a health visitor came to the house once, and the mother took the baby to a GP once. The mother had also contacted a voluntary organisation to get advice about the mortgage.

Case study F

This mother looked after her two sons, a toddler and a 7-month-old baby, with only occasional contact from their father. The mother was very concerned about her lack of money and missed her family, who lived a long distance away. She had no local friends and often felt down, 'tearful now and again' but 'able to put a front on'.

Despite a lack of social contact few formal services were used. The mother had taken the toddler out of preschool because he was so unhappy but he was 'on the go all the time'. They saw a GP for the baby's regular check-ups and had seen a health visitor once. The mother said she did not really know what services were out there. Ideally, she wanted help to move back to her family but also to improve her accommodation. She did not

(Continued)

want social services support but a babysitter would have been welcomed; once she trusted them she could 'go out … to think about me for a change'.

At the follow-up interview the family had moved to better accommodation within the same area, but was still living on social security benefits. The eldest child was now attending a day nursery half-time but there were no other regular child-care arrangements. Health services were used only slightly more frequently than at baseline. The mother had received day hospital treatment and the baby had spent 4 days in hospital following an asthma attack. The family had had a couple of contacts with a health visitor and a GP but the mother was still resisting social services involvement. She had also seen a solicitor about a car accident. She had made a couple of local friendships but she mostly continued to cope on her own.

Employment and income

Most mothers stayed at home to look after their children (56 per cent and 67 per cent, respectively, in the Study and Comparison groups). Since the baseline interviews, the rate of full-time employment had decreased and part-time employment had slightly increased, but overall few mothers worked (33 per cent in the Study group, 19 per cent in the Comparison group). Their occupations had changed a little: fewer were in managerial or professional positions and more in clerical, secretarial or sales positions, the latter catering better for part-time workers. Excluding holidays, employed mothers took 42 days off work in the 3 months before baseline, much of it maternity leave. At follow-up, they averaged 4 days leave over 3 months. There were no differences between the groups in these employment variables.

Partners' working patterns changed little over time, most (85 per cent) remaining in full-time employment. Time off work was much the same at follow-up as at baseline. However, the proportion of partners whose work was affected by family stresses was now lower for the Comparison group (falling from 26 per cent of partners affected at baseline to 16 per cent at follow-up) and particularly for the Study group (from 37 per cent to 18 per cent), possibly indicating some economic benefit from the intervention.

Earnings from employment were still the main source of income for half the families, and most single-parent families were still reliant on social security. The proportion of families supported by Home-Start with less than £200 per week from their main income source fell from 48 per cent at baseline to 37 per cent at follow-up, while the equivalent Comparison group proportion stayed the same (56 per cent and 54 per cent). These changes were due in part to mothers returning to work after maternity leave, with the shifting balance from full-time to part-time work probably also due to this development.

Service-use patterns

We asked the mothers about their families' use of services at baseline and follow-up using methods honed from previous research (see Measuring service costs).

Measuring service costs

Service use
Data on service utilisation were collected during face-to-face interviews with mothers at baseline and follow-up. An adapted version of the CSRI (Beecham and Knapp, 1992, 2001) was employed to gather data on household composition, income, employment and

(Continued)

---

service use in the previous 3 months by the mothers, their children and (separately) their partners. We asked about hospital inpatient service use over the previous 12 months, because this longer retrospective period increases the likelihood of obtaining reliable information.

Unit costs
For each service, a unit cost (for example per hour or per day) was estimated as the closest approximation to its long-run marginal opportunity cost (Beecham, 2000). These figures were drawn from various sources, including the Personal Social Services Research Unit's annual compendium (Netten *et al.*, 2001). All costs data are at 2000–01 price levels, the period over which most data were collected.

Family costs
Unit costs were multiplied by service-use frequencies and durations to calculate costs of support for each family. To facilitate comparisons between families of different sizes, costs were computed as an average per family member (mother and children).

Education and day care

The proportion of families with at least one child in primary school had increased a little by follow-up. Few children were in middle or secondary school. Six families at baseline and nine at follow-up had children attending special schools. A few families had children who were receiving extra lessons or attending after-school clubs (Table 23).

Regular childminding from extended family members or friends was reported by eight mothers at baseline, 15 at follow-up. Two families employed a nanny, and another was receiving respite help 1 day a week at baseline but no longer a year later. Mother and toddler groups were used by 20–25 per cent of the mothers at both time points.

Table 23 Education and child care service use

	Baseline		Follow-up	
	Home-Start	Comparison	Home-Start	Comparison
Service use over 3 months	group (*n* = 80)	group (*n* = 82)	group (*n* = 80)	group (*n* = 82)
	Number (%) using the service			
School (mainstream primary, middle and secondary school, special school)	31 (39)	40 (49)	38 (48)	49 (60)
School-related (after-school club, holiday scheme, extra lessons)	12 (15)	11 (13)	14 (18)	17 (21)
Early years (preschool, playgroup, day nursery, Portage Early Education Support Service)	31 (39)	30 (37)	35 (44)	35 (43)
Day care (childminder, family members, crèche, nanny, respite carer)	16 (20)	9 (11)	21 (26)	11 (13)
Mother & toddler group	21 (26)	13 (16)	20 (25)	16 (20)

Overnight services

At both baseline and follow-up, children in about 8 per cent of families spent some nights away from home, but the average number of nights away had increased from 17 nights over 3 months at baseline to 26 nights at follow-up. One Study group child had been taken into permanent foster care awaiting adoption. In the 3 months before the follow-up interview, one mother had spent 6 weeks in an alcohol rehabilitation centre.

Hospital services

Inpatient hospital use fell over time (Table 24), with fewer births (10 compared with 85 at baseline) and fewer babies admitted into special care baby units. Across the whole sample, inpatient admissions amounted to an average of 10 days for the year prior to baseline and 4 days during the follow-up period. A&E attendance rates were quite high at follow-up (35 per cent of Study group families, 21 per cent of Comparison group families). Ten families, five in each group, had called an ambulance in the 3 months prior to follow-up. Hospital outpatient and day hospital use changed little over time. There were no significant differences between Study and Comparison groups for any of these measures.

Table 24 Hospital inpatient service use

	Baseline		Follow-up	
	Home-Start	Comparison	Home-Start	Comparison
Service use over 12 months	group (*n* = 80)	group (*n* = 82)	group (*n* = 80)	group (*n* = 82)
Families with admissions, *n* (%)	57 (71)	57 (70)	40 (50)	25 (30)
Patient group/speciality, *n* (%) inpatient admissions				
Maternity (birth)	44 (36)	41 (45)	8 (10)	2 (2)
Maternity (other)	12 (10)	6 (7)	3 (4)	0
Paediatric	22 (18)	27 (29)	28 (35)	15 (18)
Special care baby unit	15 (12)	6 (7)	1 (1)	0
Mean inpatient days per annum for whole family	15	5	5	2

Table 25 Community health service use

Service use over 3 months	Baseline		Follow-up	
	Home-Start group ($n = 80$)	Comparison group ($n = 82$)	Home-Start group ($n = 80$)	Comparison group ($n = 82$)
	Number (%) using the service			
Health visitor	75 (94)	77 (94)	45 (56)	52 (63)
GP	76 (95)	78 (95)	68 (85)	72 (89)
Midwife	11 (14)	11 (13)	0	2 (2)
Dentist	31 (39)	38 (46)	41 (51)	37 (45)
Optician	16 (20)	13 (16)	19 (24)	22 (27)
Family planning	4 (5)	6 (7)	0	4 (5)
Speech therapy	8 (10)	13 (16)	9 (11)	10 (12)
Complementary therapy	10 (13)	6 (7)	3 (4)	1 (1)

Community health services

Health visitor contacts were a lot lower at follow-up compared with baseline (Table 25); fewer families used this service and the average number of contacts fell from 5.5 to 2.9. There were no differences between the Study and Comparison groups. Most families saw GPs, the rate of use falling slightly over time. The Comparison group had significantly fewer home contacts with GPs at baseline than the Home-Start group, but there was no difference at follow-up.

Mental health services

There was a slightly lower use of a number of mental health services at follow-up compared with baseline (Table 26).

Care, support and advice

Families supported by Home-Start were more likely to have received home care worker services (11 per cent compared with 4 per cent, with no change over time), and at follow-up received more frequent visits (averaging four per week compared with one per week for the Comparison group). Contacts with social workers (mostly a combination of home visits and telephone contacts) were the same for the two groups at follow-up (around 12 per cent), but families supported by Home-Start had seen this contact rate fall over the study year (from 23 per cent). A number of other community-based support services were used by small numbers of families.

About a quarter of the families had contact with a solicitor before the baseline interview, but fewer at follow-up. Few families had contact with the

Table 26 Mental health service use

Service use over 3 months	Baseline		Follow-up	
	Home-Start group ($n = 80$)	Comparison group ($n = 82$)	Home-Start group ($n = 80$)	Comparison group ($n = 82$)
	Number (%) using the service			
Community psychiatric nurse	14 (18)	7 (9)	10 (13)	6 (7)
Therapy/counselling	9 (11)	4 (5)	8 (10)	1 (1)
Psychiatrist	2 (3)	3 (4)	1 (1)	0
Educational psychologist	2 (3)	2 (2)	4 (5)	2 (2)
Child psychologist	2 (3)	2 (2)	4 (5)	1 (1)

police in either period. Six families at baseline and four at follow-up had a member appearing in court.

There was therefore a suggestion that Home-Start volunteers might have been substituting for other services, illustrated by a reduction in social worker contacts, although caution should be exercised in drawing conclusions from this finding. If valid, this kind of substitution effect would lead to relatively lower costs for the Study group, but there is also evidence that volunteers may have helped families to access services that they needed but were not previously using. This kind of empowering support would lead to relatively higher costs.

Support from informal sources

Mothers were asked about the support they sought from informal services. At baseline, about half the mothers reported 'often' turning to friends and relatives (Table 27). Mothers in the Home-Start group made more use of friends and relatives for advice at follow-up than the Comparison group, and the difference was statistically significant. There had been no difference between the groups at baseline. It is possible that the volunteers were considered friends to whom mothers could turn for advice, or people who helped with household tasks to give mothers more time for child-centred activities. Or perhaps Home-Start had reinforced the mothers' trust in others, making it easier for them to turn to other people when in need.

Partners' service use

Use of services by partners was quite low. Between a quarter and a fifth of all partners had seen GPs and/or dentists at each time point. Some partners (10 per cent at baseline, 4 per cent at follow-up) had been to A&E, some (9 per cent at baseline, 10 per cent at follow-up) had used other hospital outpatient services, and only three partners at each time point had stayed overnight in hospital.

Support costs

Service-use costs

We calculated a unit cost for each service and calculated the overall costs of supporting each family (see Measuring service costs). The average costs for different service types are presented in Figure 11.

The groups did not differ in any of the costs for education and child-care services at either time point. There was an increase in all education and child-care costs at the follow-up stage, probably reflecting the increasing age of children in the sample and that some mothers had returned to work.

A large proportion of the total support costs was for hospital services. At baseline the hospital costs for the Study group were significantly higher than for the Comparison group, mainly reflecting the higher use of maternity services. Hospital service costs were lower at follow-up, and the difference between the groups had disappeared.

Table 27 Informal support

| | Baseline | | Follow-up | |
| | Home-Start | Comparison | Home-Start | Comparison |
Support use over 3 months	group (n = 80)	group (n = 82)	group (n = 80)	group (n = 82)
Number (%) who 'often' sought advice from:				
Friends and relatives	47 (59)	37 (45)	44 (55)	29 (35)
Community groups	1 (1)	2 (2)	4 (5)	4 (5)
Books and magazines	25 (31)	23 (28)	26 (33)	23 (28)
Internet websites	5 (6)	1 (1)	0	3 (4)
Telephone helplines	0	0	0	1 (1)

Figure 11 Cost per family at baseline and follow-up (3 months). H-S, Home-Start; C, Comparison group.

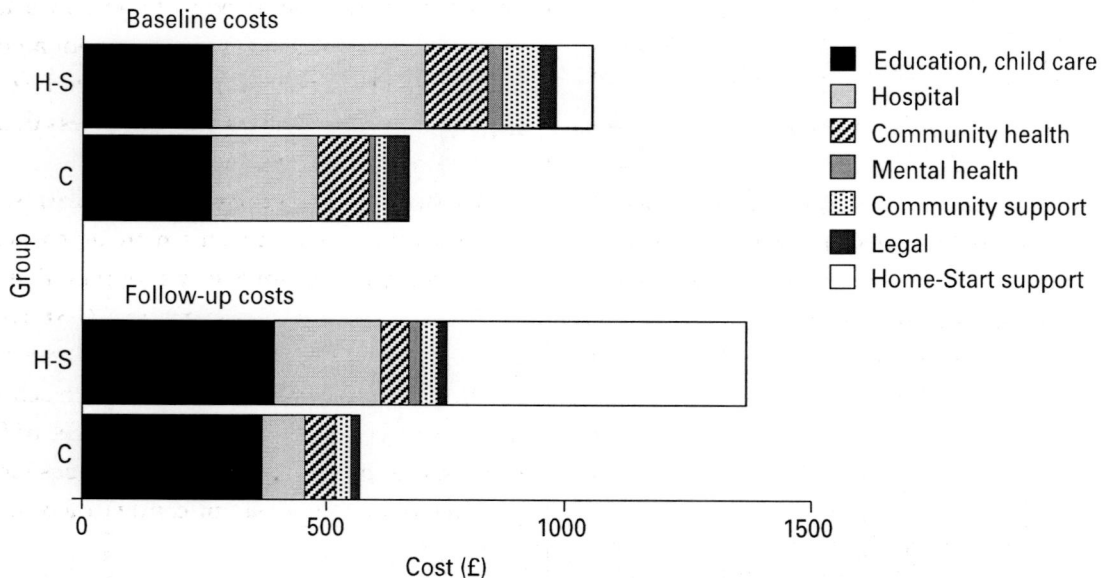

Community health services costs did not differ between the groups at baseline or follow-up, and for both groups the costs at follow-up were about half those at baseline. Adult mental health service costs were significantly higher for the Study group at both baseline and follow-up.

The costs of Home-Start support are also shown in Figure 11 on the assumption that volunteer costs are set to zero. In fact, we examined three different ways of attaching a cost to volunteers (see Costs of Home-Start). When volunteers were given a cost of zero, the mean cost of Home-Start per family was £76 at baseline (because our first interview with families was sometimes after Home-Start had actually begun) and £621 at follow-up. If a non-zero replacement cost was assumed for volunteers, equal to the cost of a local authority family support worker, the 3-month mean Home-Start cost per family became £284 at baseline and £2147 at follow-up.

Costs of Home-Start

Data collection
Information on Home-Start came from several sources, most importantly a short questionnaire completed by scheme organisers. Questions were asked about how schemes ran their service, specific cost information and related details. Each scheme provided its 2001–02 expenditure accounts and annual report.

VAFs were completed up to three times by each volunteer supporting a participating family, covering retrospective 1-month periods. The questionnaire provided data on number and duration of visits to families and travelling time. Management committee inputs were not costed.

Costing schemes
Our methodology ensured that all costs were included for each scheme and that each cost element was treated consistently. Expenditure accounts and other information allowed us to estimate short-run revenue costs, and an

(Continued)

allowance was made for capital (Beecham, 2000). As the focus of the present study was home visiting by volunteers, adjustments were made to exclude costs associated with other activities, such as family groups.

Costs were calculated for individual schemes. The mean annual total cost per scheme was £55,661, mean cost per active volunteer £2240, mean cost per family supported over the year £995, and mean cost per home visit £22.

Volunteer visitor costs

Volunteers are unpaid, but there are associated opportunity costs. We employed three alternative cost estimates for volunteers, one set to zero and the other two estimating their replacement with paid staff undertaking similar tasks (home care workers or family support workers), unit costs for which were taken from Netten *et al.* (2001).

Cost aggregation

Three ways could be used to aggregate costs for a family:

- total costs included all support costs, covering all formal services and the costs of Home-Start
- mainstream costs included the costs of all formal services but excluded costs associated with the provision of Home-Start
- partial costs measured the costs of support excluding Home-Start and excluding costs associated with differences between groups in the number of hospital admissions (inpatient costs) and number of school-aged children in each family (school-related costs).

Total costs

Total costs are summarised in Table 28. Costs for partners are presented separately as not all mothers in the study had partners. On average, the cost of services used by partners was much less than for other family members.

We distinguished three cost measures (see Cost aggregation). At baseline, mainstream costs were significantly higher for Study group families (mean £971) than the Comparison group (£668). The between-group comparison of partial costs was predicated on the assumption that both school and inpatient service use were consequences of factors outside the control of Home-Start. At baseline, partial costs were not significantly different between the groups.

A different pattern emerged at follow-up. Mainstream costs (still excluding Home-Start) were not statistically different between the groups, but when inpatient and school costs were also excluded, these partial costs were significantly higher for families supported by Home-Start. When we included the costs of Home-Start support received before baseline (during the period between a successful 'match' between family and volunteer and our baseline interview), the total costs for the Study group were significantly higher than for the Comparison group (regardless of the unit cost attached to Home-Start volunteers). The between-group difference in total costs was especially pronounced at the follow-up stage.

Table 28 Total costs

	Baseline		Follow-up	
	Home-Start	Comparison	Home-Start	Comparison
Service use over 3 months	group ($n = 80$)	group ($n = 82$)	group ($n = 80$)	group ($n = 82$)
	Mean cost: £ (range)			
Total cost for partners[1]	51	119	56	70
Total cost for mother and children, adjusted for family sizes				
Excluding Home-Start costs	971	668	750	566
Including Home-Start cost A[2]	1047	–	1371	–
Including Home-Start cost B[2]	160	–	2200	–
Including Home-Start cost C[2]	1255	–	2897	–
Total cost for mother and children, excluding inpatient and school costs, adjusted for family sizes				
Excluding Home-Start costs	433	330	376	250
Including Home-Start cost A[2]	510	–	997	–
Including Home-Start cost B[2]	622	–	1826	–
Including Home-Start cost C[2]	717	–	2523	–

1 Mean cost for partners calculated only for families where the mother had a partner living in the household.
2 Three different costs for Home-Start volunteers were examined: cost A, assumes zero cost for volunteer time; cost B, organisational cost plus the cost of replacing volunteers with home care workers (£8.69 per hour); cost C, organisational cost plus the cost of replacing volunteers with family support workers (£16 per hour).

Cost variations between families

As noted earlier, there were quite wide variations in costs between families within each of the two groups. We examined whether those cost variations reflected differences in the characteristics and needs of families.

Multivariate analyses were first conducted to examine the extent to which the baseline costs of supporting families were associated with family characteristics, needs and well-being assessed at baseline. Second, we examined whether there were associations between baseline characteristics and follow-up period costs. Potential influences on costs included in these analyses were the standardised measures of well-being of mothers and children described in Chapter 3, various proxy measures of need (number of children with special needs, predominant reason for referral, degree to which mothers sought support from informal sources) and demographic characteristics (gender and ages of the children, mother's age, mother's

education), mother's employment, family income and country. We were obviously also interested in whether group membership (Study or Comparison) influenced costs, and added a dummy variable for group membership (was the family supported by Home-Start or not). The techniques used to explore these relationships were ordinary least squares (OLS) and generalised linear model (GLM) regressions, the two approaches producing very similar results (Wooldridge, 2002).

Baseline cost variations

We started by looking at the total baseline cost per family (mother and children), adjusted for the number of children in the family. Although baseline interviews were held as soon as possible after families were matched with a Home-Start volunteer, most families had received visits from their volunteers prior to the interviews. We assumed zero replacement cost for volunteer time (see above).

Only four family measures were related to costs: seeking help from community groups, number of children with special needs, reason for referral and maternal self-esteem. Costs were higher where mothers reported at baseline that they sought support from community groups, perhaps because they were more willing to seek help from both informal and formal sources. Number of children with special needs also significantly raised costs, not surprising given the additional health and support services required (see, for example, case study A).

Where the main reason for referral was because the mother felt isolated or lonely, the costs were lower. As illustrated by case study F, isolated mothers may have difficulty in forming relationships and then are less likely to seek help from formal services. Conversely, their difficulties in accessing support may have contributed to their feelings of isolation and loneliness.

The only standardised measure of well-being that significantly influenced costs was the RSE. Higher costs were associated with higher RSE scores (representing lower self-esteem). Other things being equal, mothers with low self-esteem appeared to be receiving more support from formal health and social services.

Together, these four baseline variables 'explained' only 14 per cent of the observed variation in costs. In other words, a great deal of the cost variation within the sample could not be attributed to the characteristics, circumstances and needs of families measured in this study. Services clearly were targeted to some degree by needs, as indicated, for example, by the significant associations between costs and the number of children in the family with special needs, but the overall impression was of considerable variation in service use (and costs) without apparent links to family circumstances.

At the second stage, when we added a variable to indicate whether or not the family had been supported by Home-Start, the proportion of explained cost variation increased slightly (by 5 per cent). However, the group indicator was itself statistically significant, implying that, even after taking into account family characteristics and needs, those families in the Home-Start group had higher total costs at baseline (the difference, after this standardisation, was £312). One reason for this cost difference is the prebaseline receipt of Home-Start, but two other possible explanations must be considered. First, there are almost certainly family characteristics and needs not measured in this study (or not adequately captured by the research instrumentation) that raise or lower costs. Second, given that the Home-Start and Comparison group families are drawn from different localities, there may be area effects, such as a greater or lesser availability of certain services or differences in the willingness and (self-perceived) ability of families to seek help.

The third stage of the analysis, including the group membership dummy variable from the outset, produced results that were not materially different from those described above.

Follow-up cost variations

The same statistical procedures were applied to look at variations between families in follow-up costs. Again our interest was in the links with baseline measures of family characteristics, circumstances and well-being, so that we were effectively examining how well these factors could predict differences in costs 11 months later. The same three-stage estimation strategy was employed as with the earlier analyses of baseline costs.

The first stage equation explained only 9 per cent of the observed cost variation. Four family variables were found to be significant predictors of follow-up costs. One of those variables had also been important in understanding variations in baseline costs: the number of children with special needs. We also found that the age of the oldest child was positively associated with costs, partly picking up the greater education costs but also possibly reflecting family size. A higher level of depressive symptoms, as measured by the EPDS at baseline, was associated with higher costs. Finally, and counter-intuitively, a higher parental distress score at baseline was associated with lower costs at follow-up. However, further examination of the data showed that the parental distress score was strongly negatively correlated with the EPDS score, so that the regression equation was having difficulty disentangling their respective effects.

When the group membership indicator variable was added, the proportion of explained cost variance leapt from 9 per cent to 34 per cent. Again group membership was found to be an important cost predictor. After adjusting for family characteristics at baseline, families supported by Home-Start were found to have costs that were on average £285 greater than the costs for families in the Comparison group over a 3-month period.

The third analysis stage found all of the above variables to be significant cost predictors, but two other baseline variables were also found to be associated with follow-up costs. One of these was a measure of household income, suggesting that families with lower income received greater service support. The other new variable indicated whether the family 'sometimes' or 'often' sought support from community groups, which was associated with lower costs. The group membership effect on costs was larger with this analysis (£840 over 3 months).

The low proportions of observed cost variation associated with family needs and characteristics, at both baseline and follow-up, suggest that some cost or service-use variation could be random, that service-use levels may not have been accurately measured, that family needs may also not have been sufficiently well identified or measured, or simply that services do not respond particularly well to needs.

Home-Start cost variations

Given the focus of this study, we also examined the pattern of variations between families in the costs of Home-Start support during the follow-up period. The statistical analyses were obviously carried out only for the Home-Start group.

We first set volunteer costs to zero, so that our analysis was effectively examining variation in organisation costs. The regression analyses showed that seven family factors were associated with costs, together explaining 22 per cent of the variance. The greater the age of the oldest child and the greater the number of children under 5, the higher the costs. Families living in owner-occupied housing had lower costs. If mothers had 'often' or 'sometimes' sought advice from books or magazines, costs were higher. Two measures of maternal well-being were significant: costs were higher when mothers had greater depressive symptoms and when they were less distressed. As with the total cost analysis, the latter association is counter-intuitive but is probably due to the close correlation between these two well-being measures and the difficulties of disentangling their respective effects. Finally, costs were higher for Northern Ireland families, other things being equal, almost certainly because Home-Start schemes are smaller than in England and therefore do not enjoy the same economies of scale (see below).

A second analysis looked at the Home-Start organisation costs plus volunteers costed as (paid) family support workers. This analysis therefore allowed us to see if the intensity of Home-Start support of a particular family (reflected in the number of hours received over 11 months) was linked to the characteristics and needs of the family. Four variables were now significantly associated with Home-Start costs, together accounting for 15 per cent of the cost variation. Costs were higher for families with more children with special needs, and lower the greater the age of the youngest child. As with the previous analysis, costs were higher when mothers had more depressive symptoms, and now also higher when mothers were assessed as more defensive. An impression gained during data collection was that the more defensive mothers had very high levels of need, tended to avoid professional input, but developed good and long-lasting relationships with their volunteers.

In supplementary analyses we looked at Home-Start costs at the scheme level. The schemes included in the study in south-east England and Northern Ireland were at different stages of development (some newly established, others longer established) and varied greatly in scale (from 14 families supported in a year in one scheme to 229 families in another). Two schemes supported families for, on average, 7 months, compared with another scheme for which the average duration was 15 months. We found that the average cost per supported family (for the scheme as a whole) was strongly negatively related to the number of families supported during the year. It was clear that almost all of the Home-Start schemes covered by this study were operating at a scale that meant that their operational costs were quite high. This says nothing about each scheme's effectiveness, and it does not imply that schemes should merge, because they need to be closely linked to the populations they serve, but the small scale of operation of some groups clearly contributed to their relatively high costs.

Discussion

In this chapter we have described the economic circumstances, service-use patterns and support costs for families in the 3-month period before the baseline and follow-up interviews. There were some changes in employment patterns over time, and fewer partners in the Home-Start group (but not in the Comparison group) had their work affected by stressful family events in the follow-up period. Families in the Home-Start group also tended to make more use of advice from friends and relatives than the Comparison group at the follow-up stage, perhaps because the volunteers had reinforced their trust in others.

Costs were attached to the service-use data. At baseline there were few differences between Study and Comparison groups, particularly after excluding cost elements corresponding to services related to childbirth and regular schooling. At follow-up, what we called the partial support costs were higher for the Study group. Including all services and supports, costs for families supported by Home-Start were significantly higher than those for Comparison group families, and these differences persisted after statistical adjustment for measured differences in the baseline characteristics, circumstances and needs of families. A number of interesting relationships were found between the costs of supporting families and those families' needs and circumstances. Cost-raising factors included children with special needs, referral because of mothers' isolation or loneliness, mothers' low self-esteem, age of the oldest children, mothers seeking help from community groups, low family incomes, postnatal depression and lower parental distress. However, most of the cost variation could not be explained by child or family characteristics. Our finding that a variable indicating whether mothers sought support from informal sources was a better cost predictor than most of the standardised well-being measures could suggest that service utilisation is affected more by whether mothers actively seek help than by the families' actual underlying needs. Families where the mother is suffering from depressive symptoms, isolation or low self-esteem might be less well placed to seek support proactively.

8 Cost-effectiveness

Introduction

Why should we be interested in the cost-effectiveness of interventions to support young families in stress? One reason is that the costs of supporting families can be quite high and can fall quite widely, for example on social care services, the health service and the education system. There could also be wider impacts on the national economy through lost employment, as well as costs for families themselves, although we did not measure them in cost terms in this study. Another reason for interest is because available services are insufficient to meet all needs. It is the pervasive scarcity of resources that necessitates choices between alternative uses. Cost-effectiveness analyses are intended to inform such choices alongside other considerations, such as agencies' priorities concerning service targeting, the urgency of families' needs and the preferences of family members.

In this chapter we examine the cost-effectiveness of Home-Start support compared with standard available services, integrating the findings on outcomes and costs. A cost-effectiveness question asks whether the services achieve improvements in mother and child welfare at a cost that is worth paying. We must emphasise that cost-effectiveness analysis does what its name suggests: it looks at both costs and effectiveness (outcomes).

Cost-effectiveness: putting principles into practice

There are a number of different types of economic evaluation, each looking at the relationships between costs and outcomes. The most intuitive and straightforward are cost-effectiveness analysis and cost-consequences analysis. We used both here. Both focus on outcome dimensions (such as family stress and maternal well-being) of the kind suggested by practice, policy and previous research to be relevant, measured using familiar scales (see Chapter 1 and Appendix 2).

We do not detail the conceptual bases of the analyses here. The foundations of economic evaluation of social care services are set out in Knapp (1984). More recently, Byford *et al.* (2003) and Sefton *et al.* (2002) describe economic evaluation methods in the social welfare area.

A cost-effectiveness analysis, in strict usage of the term, computes the ratio of the difference in costs between two interventions to the difference in the primary outcome measure. Such a ratio could be computed for each outcome measure in turn, for example the ratio of the difference in follow-up cost between Study and Comparison groups divided by the difference in improvement on the RSE. If one intervention is both more effective and less costly (or is exactly equivalent in one of these respects), it is not necessary to compute ratios.

A somewhat looser form of economic evaluation is cost-consequences analysis, which pulls together all the cost and outcome results (including qualitative evidence) for two interventions for consideration by decision makers. This approach has the ability to evaluate policies and practices in a way that arguably comes close to everyday reality, as decision makers are used to having to weigh up disparate types of evidence. But compared with a formal cost-effectiveness analysis, the cost-consequences approach has the disadvantage of a much less tidy and transparent decision calculus.

Adjustments of costs for baseline characteristics

In the previous chapter we reported the finding that costs were significantly higher for the families supported by Home-Start than for those in the Comparison group. However, even though we also found very few differences at baseline between the groups in terms of family characteristics and circumstances or in service-use patterns, it is still possible that the between-group cost difference might be reflecting some differences between the samples. We therefore needed to explore whether family characteristics were associated with differences in costs, and to make appropriate adjustments before making comparisons.

We used two methods, OLS and GLM, to estimate regression equations linking follow-up costs to baseline family characteristics, including measures of child and family well-being and whether or not they were supported by Home-Start. This served two purposes. First, it showed to what extent costs over the follow-up period (and hence the services they represent) were related to family characteristics. Second, the estimated coefficient on the Home-Start 'dummy variable' in the regression equation could be interpreted as measuring the adjusted cost difference between the groups.

In Chapter 7 we described how different monetary costs could be attached to volunteer time, depending on the assumptions made about the motivations of volunteers and the possibilities of replacing them with paid staff. Three alternative values were presented, one set to zero, another to the (replacement) cost of a local authority home care worker and the third to the (replacement) cost of a family support worker. When conducting the regression analyses and adjustments we focused on the highest (family support worker) and lowest (zero) costs. We also focused exclusively on the total cost measure.

One final adjustment was to calculate the average cost per month from the follow-up data and multiply it by 11.4 months, this being the mean time elapsed between the baseline and follow-up interviews across the full sample.

Cost-effectiveness: the findings

Cost differences

Table 29 summarises the costs presented in Chapter 7 converted to an 11-month period. With volunteer costs set to zero, the cost of the Home-Start group was £3058 greater than the cost of the Comparison group. When the costs of volunteers were set at the replacement cost of a family support worker, the differences were much wider.

The two statistical methods for adjusting costs before making comparisons between groups produced very similar results. On average, families supported by Home-Start cost £3193 more than Comparison group families when volunteer costs were set to zero, and a much larger difference (£8831) when volunteer time was set to the cost of employing a family support worker.

Effectiveness differences

Effectiveness was measured as the difference between the score on a particular scale at baseline and the equivalent score at follow-up, and for the present evaluation we wanted to compare these differences for the Study and Comparison groups. The outcome findings from the questionnaire data presented in Chapter 5, covering parenting stress, depression, self-esteem and social support, indicated that none of the differences between the Study and Comparison groups was statistically significant.

Cost-effectiveness

Given these results it is not necessary to compute the incremental cost-effectiveness ratios because there are no effectiveness differences between the

Table 29 Estimated cost differences between the groups

Cost measure, mean cost (£)	Baseline (3 months)			Follow-up (11 months)		
	Home-Start	Comparison	Difference	Home-Start	Comparison	Difference
			Unadjusted total costs			
Volunteer time costed as zero	510	330	180	5209	2151	3058
Volunteer time costed as family support worker	717	330	387	11008	2151	8857

groups and significantly lower costs for the Comparison group. Home-Start does not appear to be a cost-effective alternative to standard health visitor-based services.

Cost-consequences: the findings

The same conclusion would be reached from a cost-consequences analysis, even though the qualitative evidence in Chapter 6 suggested that families in the Study group expressed positive views about how Home-Start had made a difference to the stresses they had been experiencing.

Discussion

The cost-effectiveness analysis pulled together the quantitative outcome results and the cost findings. Costs were significantly higher for the Home-Start group, even after adjustment for baseline factors, without compensating advantages in terms of better quantitative outcomes. The cost-consequences approach allowed us to include the qualitative evidence, which certainly suggested that mothers greatly valued the support and friendship received from volunteers.

The inputs from Home-Start are quite modest in the context of what are clearly complex and often deep-seated family needs reported by mothers. They all had young families, many had children with special needs, and a number were single parents or had strained relationships with their partners. Low family income was the norm, not the exception. Some were living in overcrowded accommodation. Many mothers exhibited depressive symptoms, and many of their children had health or developmental problems. Yet few mothers were able to access sufficient day-to-day support from their partners, their families or formal services. Many of the factors contributing to the stresses experienced by these mothers were still there at the time of the follow-up interviews, and so perhaps only modest outcome improvements should have been expected over 11 months. Families may be helped through short-term crises, and the foundations may be laid for meeting their needs over the longer term, which is perhaps one reason for the expressed satisfaction with Home-Start support, but no changes in well-being were identified in the follow-up period used in this study.

9 Conclusion

The aim of this study was to evaluate the outcomes and costs of Home-Start support to young families in the community who were experiencing stress. The Joseph Rowntree Foundation commissioned this study as part of an initiative on outcomes and costs of preventive services. More recently the Department of Health has also funded a number of studies of the cost-effectiveness of services for children in need. The research was commissioned in a context of concern by policy makers that children and families should be receiving services that make a positive difference to their lives and are cost-effective.

In any study of effectiveness, a design is needed that allows separation of the differences made by the service from those that occur naturally over time or result from other factors. We therefore recruited a Study group of young families who received Home-Start support and a Comparison group of young families who did not. Provided that the families in both groups were similar and the only major difference in support over time was the provision of Home-Start to the former, any differences in progress are likely to be attributable to that support.

In this study we followed 162 families over time. The 80 Study and 82 Comparison families in the community were found to be remarkably well matched, not only regarding demographic variables but also regarding maternal needs at the outset. What was noticeable were the high levels of need of the majority of mothers in both groups. These mothers were experiencing a high level of parenting stress and were exhibiting a high level of depressive symptoms. Problems with the emotional and social development of their children were evident. Unfortunately these mothers appeared to have little support. There were also very few differences between the groups in the services being received prior to the start of the research.

From the initial interviews we learnt a great deal about the day-to-day lives of these young families in the community. The stresses the mothers were facing were multiple and interconnected and impacted upon their capacity to parent. Many of the mothers had experienced considerable trauma related to pregnancy and birth and the transition to parenthood generally had not been a smooth one. Often the children had health or developmental problems that were a concern and required additional time and care. While most of the mothers were not lone parents, their husbands/partners were at work and the daily responsibility for caring for the children appeared to fall upon the mothers. There was a strong sense of these mothers being overwhelmed at times by the intensity of the demands being placed upon them, particularly when trying to care for several children on their own. What seemed to make the situation particularly stressful was the lack of respite.

The prevalence of depressive symptoms among the mothers was surprising and much more widespread than the initial referrals would have indicated. Many mothers described having moderate to severe symptoms, some were on long-term medication and some had spent periods in psychiatric hospitals. A few indicated that they had attempted suicide or had suicidal thoughts. While there was evidence of contacts with community psychiatric nurses and occasional appointments with psychiatrists, there was very little evidence of other support. A small number of mothers had been offered counselling but few mentioned postnatal depression support groups or indeed help from organisations specifically interested in mental well-being.

Overall these mothers had little available support. There was a variety of reasons for this. Some mothers lived some distance away from their extended families, and the families of some others could not offer support as they had their own health or other problems. Occasionally the relationships with families were fractured. Quite a few of these mothers were in the process of separation or divorce, and at times there was aggression and conflict during contact with former partners. There was little evidence of shared responsibility for parenting with estranged spouses. These mothers may have turned to professionals such as health visitors for advice but they were generally not in receipt of other forms of family support.

Although we used a broad definition of special needs, we were surprised that almost three-quarters of the mothers had concerns about the health or development of their children. Needs ranged broadly from childhood asthma and behaviour problems to autism. We learned about the particular anxiety surrounding diagnosis, which often brought a sense of relief mixed with sadness. These mothers reported considerable difficulties in having their initial concerns taken seriously by professionals and then lengthy periods before they knew the outcome of investigations. Attending multiple appointments with specialists in distant hospitals posed particular problems for many of the mothers who did not have transport or indeed anyone to accompany them with several young children.

Another major source of stress for these mothers was finance. Many were finding it difficult to decide whether to return to work and were highly critical of the lack of affordable child-care facilities to make this feasible. Many mothers, particularly those who were lone parents, were worried about their families' financial situation. They could only afford the basics and were unable to give their children treats or take them on holidays. Several mothers were in debt.

Home-Start offered volunteer home visiting support to the Study families on average for 2.5 hours per week. The volunteers generally offered a combination of emotional support, practical assistance and help with outings. They tended to provide more emotional support at the beginning and more help with outings in the latter months. Practical assistance remained fairly constant throughout. The average length of support was 9 months, although the number of visits per month

diminished over time.

At follow-up, approximately 11 months after we first interviewed them, the majority of the mothers in both the Study and Comparison groups had much improved situations. They were experiencing less parenting stress and exhibiting fewer depressive symptoms. They had higher self-esteem and there was evidence of improvement in the emotional and social development of their children. They also had more social support. The progress was evident not only from the improvement on all the outcome measures but also from the content of the interviews with the mothers. However, mothers in both groups showed similar levels of improvement. As there was no evidence of any other comparable family support service being received by the Comparison group in between interviews, we were keen to uncover the factors that had brought about these changes.

The Study mothers were also asked about the impact of the Home-Start service. Four-fifths of the mothers stated that Home-Start had made a difference to the stresses they had been experiencing. In general, the service helped to provide a sense of relief from overwhelming pressure and most mothers clearly valued the support and friendship offered by the volunteers. However, many mothers felt that the intensity of the service was insufficient to make a significant difference to the stresses they were experiencing.

The interviews with the mothers suggested that these improvements were due to a number of factors. Many of the issues relating to the transition to parenthood were resolved through time and experience. Many of the short-term health problems of the mothers and babies were no longer present. There was evidence of the mothers gaining in confidence as parents. They had established routines to manage competing demands and had made decisions about their priorities. In many ways, they seemed to have regained control over their lives. Some had returned to work, which resulted in regaining their work status, an improved financial situation and more equitable sharing of parental responsibilities. An important change for many mothers was that their children were older, more independent and often attending playgroups or schools, giving the mothers some respite from the daily demands of family life. Furthermore, those who had been experiencing fraught relationships with ex-husbands/ex-partners stated that the issues were largely resolved following court decisions about contact and financial support.

Many of the families were using quite a number of health, education and other services before the research started. Most of these service contacts continued during the research period. Overall, the receipt of Home-Start did not alter the costs of formal service use. At follow-up, there were no differences in formal service costs between the Study and Comparison groups. However, the total costs for the Study group were higher due to the additional costs of the Home-Start support.

There are a number of conclusions that can be drawn from these findings.

- Parenting young, dependent children can be extremely demanding, particularly if the family is experiencing multiple stresses.

- The transition to parenthood can be a period of particular vulnerability.

- Families in this study generally had a high level of need whilst the availability of affordable support/respite was low. This resulted in the mothers feeling under considerable stress.

- Home-Start was often the only non-statutory service available and was being used in the absence of other mental health or family support services.

- The mothers improved in well-being over time, primarily as a result of major life changes and adaptations.

- Mothers who received the support of a Home-Start volunteer when they were experiencing such stress valued the service and considered that it had made a positive difference to their lives.

- The results on the quantitative outcome measures, however, did not support the view that Home-Start had made a significant difference to the mothers over the 11-month period of the research, relative to the experiences of the families in the Comparison group. Interviews with the mothers suggested that the intensity and type of support may have contributed to this.

- Although many families were not accessing the services they clearly needed, for a variety of reasons, the costs of supporting young families experiencing stress are still quite high, with the costs spread across a number of agencies.

- Even though the support may have been less intensive than some mothers would have wished, the receipt of Home-Start services nevertheless pushed costs for the Study group to a higher level relative to the Comparison group. Combined with the outcome results, the evidence does not therefore point to a cost-effectiveness advantage for Home-Start.

A number of important points remain to be made. The Department of Health has yet to report on the results of its studies on cost-effectiveness of services to children in need. When these become available, we will then be in a much better position to view the findings of this study in the context of the wider picture about such services. Our understanding about support services for children and families and how best to evaluate their effectiveness is clearly at an early stage in the UK (McAuley et al., 2004). There is also very little empirical work in the UK on the cost-effectiveness of interventions (Knapp and Lowin, 1998), and the calculation of service costs is still at a rudimentary stage (Beecham, 2000) The results of these related studies should provide the basis for advancing our thinking in this complex area.

The follow-up period of 11 months might be argued to be too brief for evidence of effectiveness to be expected, particularly for a community-based initiative such as Home-Start that does not aim to provide a structured, intensive programme. The impact of this type of intervention may be more apparent after a longer period. As a consequence, there would appear to be grounds for considering a follow-up study of at least a selected sample of both groups of families.

What would be regrettable is if policy makers and managers were to read the results and allow them to affect the funding for Home-Start. We would refer them to the detailed comments of the mothers who used the service. These stressed mothers clearly valued the support of the volunteers. This is in line with the satisfaction of parents expressed in earlier studies of Home-Start throughout its 30 years' experience of supporting families.

Nevertheless, this research will allow Home-Start to reflect on the needs of the families it serves, the ways in which it supports them and the implications for staff training. It will also provide Home-Start with the opportunity to consider the costs of its services. Home-Start has already expressed interest in what it has heard from the mothers about their need for regular respite and for more intensive support. We would hope that the overall findings will be helpful to Home-Start and others for future planning.

References

Abidin, R.R. (1995) *Parenting Stress Index: Professional Manual*, third edition. Odessa, FL: Psychological Assessment Resources Inc.

Audit Commission (1994) *Seen But Not Heard*. London: The Stationery Office

Beecham, J. (2000) *Unit Costs: Not Exactly Child's Play*. London: Department of Health

Beecham, J. and Knapp, M. (1992, 2001) 'Costing psychiatric interventions', in G. Thornicroft (ed.) *Measuring Mental Health Needs*, pp. 179–90. London: Gaskill

Briggs-Gowan, M.J. and Carter, A.S. (2001) *The Brief Infant–Toddler Social and Emotional Assessment (BITSEA) Manual*. New Haven, CT: Department of Psychology, Yale University

Byford, S., McDaid, D. and Sefton, T. (2003) *Because It's Worth It: A Practical Guide to Conducting Economic Evaluations in the Social Welfare Field*. York: Joseph Rowntree Foundation

Carter, A.S. and Briggs-Gowan, M.J. (2000) *Infant–Toddler Social and Emotional Assessment (ITSEA) Manual*. New Haven, CT: Department of Psychology, Yale University

Cox, J., Holder, J. and Sagovsky, R. (1987) 'Detection of postnatal depression. Development of the ten-item Edinburgh, postnatal depression scale', *British Journal of Psychiatry*, Vol. 150, pp. 782–86

Cullen, J. and Hills, D. (1996) *Assessing effectiveness of new service provision*. Unpublished report. York: Joseph Rowntree Foundation

DfES (2003) *Every Child Matters*. Government Green Paper. London: The Stationery Office

DH/SSI (1996) *Make a Difference: The Government's Actions*. London: Department of Health

Frost, N., Johnston, L., Stein, M. and Wallis, L. (1996) *Negotiated Friendship: Home-Start and the Delivery of Family Support*. Leicester: Home-Start

Ghate, D. (2001) 'Community-based evaluations in the UK: scientific concerns and practical constraints', *Children and Society*, Vol. 15, Special edition, p. 1

Gibbons, J. and Thorpe, S. (1989) 'Can voluntary support projects help vulnerable families? The work of Home-Start', *British Journal of Social Work*, Vol. 19, pp. 189–202

Hill, M. (ed.) (1999) *Effective Ways of Working with Children and Families*. London: Jessica Kingsley

Home-Start (2003) *Home-Start UK Annual Statistics*. Leicester: Home-Start

Knapp, M. (1984) *The Economics of Social Care*. London: Macmillan

Knapp, M. and Lowin, A. (1998) 'Child care outcomes: economic perspectives and issues', *Children and Society*, Vol. 12, Issue 3, pp. 169–79

Lewis, J. and Utting, D. (2001) 'Made to measure? Evaluating community initiatives for children', *Children and Society*, Vol. 15, Special edition, p. 1

McAuley, C. (1999) *The Family Support Outcomes Study*. Ballymena: Northern Health and Social Services Board

McAuley, C, Pecora, P. and Rose, W. (2004) *Enhancing the Well-Being of Children and Families Through Effective Interventions: UK and USA Evidence for Practice*. London: Jessica Kingsley

McNeish, D., Newman, T. and Roberts, H. (2002) *What Works for Children?* Buckingham: Open University Press

MacDonald, G. (1996) 'Ice therapy: why we need randomised controlled trials', in P. Alderson, S. Brill, I. Chalmers, R. Fuller, P. Hinkley-Smith, G. MacDonald, T. Newman, A. Oakley, H. Roberts and H. Ward (eds) *What Works? Effective Social Interventions in Child Welfare*. Barkingside: Barnardo's, SSRU

Netten, A., Rees, T. and Harrison, G. (2001) *The Unit Costs of Health and Social Care 2001*. Canterbury: Personal Social Services Research Unit

Oakley, A. (1996) 'Who's afraid of the randomised controlled trial? The challenge of evaluating the potential of social interventions', in P. Alderson, S. Brill, I. Chalmers, R. Fuller, P. Hinkley-Smith, G. MacDonald, T. Newman, A. Oakley, H. Roberts and H. Ward (eds) *What Works? Effective Social Interventions in Child Welfare*. Barkingside: Barnardo's, SSRU

Office of National Statistics (2001) *Social Trends*. London: Stationery Office

Parker, R. (1998) 'Reflections on the assessment of outcomes in child care', *Children and Society*, Vol. 12, Issue 3, pp. 192–201

Pascoe, J.M., Ialonga, N., Hom, W., Reinhart, M.A. and Perradatto, D. (1988) 'The reliability and validity of the maternal social support index', *Family Medicine*, Vol. 20, Issue 4, pp. 271–5

Pecora, P., Fraser, M., Nelson, K., McCroskey, J. and Meezan, W. (1995) *Evaluating Family Based Services*. New York, NY: Aldine de Gruyter

Radloff, L. (1977) 'The CES-D scale: a self-report depression scale for research in the general population', *Applied Psychological Measurement*, Vol. 1, pp. 385–401

Rajan, L., Turner, H. and Oakley, A. (1996) *A study of Home-Start*. Unpublished report. London: SSRU, Institute of Education

Rosenberg, M. (1965) *Society and the Adolescent Self-Image*. Princeton, NJ: Princeton University Press

Rosenberg, M. (1989) *Society and the Adolescent Self-Image*, reprint edition. Middletown, CT: Wesleyan University Press

Sefton, T., Byford, S., McDaid, D., Hills, J. and Knapp, M. (2002) *Making the Most of It: Economic Evaluation in the Social Welfare Field*. York: York Publishing Services for the Joseph Rowntree Foundation

Shinman, S. (1994) *Family Album*. Leicester: Home-Start

Social Research Association (2003) *Ethical Guidelines*. London: Social Research Association

Tunstill, J. and Aldgate, J. (2000) *From Policy to Practice*. London: The Stationery Office

Van der Eyken, W. (1982) *Home-Start: A Four Year Evaluation*. Leicester: Home-Start

Wooldridge, J. M. (2002) *Econometric Analysis of Cross Section and Panel Data*. Cambridge, MA: MIT Press

Appendix 1

Home-Start standards and methods of practice

Each Home-Start scheme is an independent voluntary organisation that works towards the increased confidence and independence of the family by:

- offering support, friendship and practical help

- visiting a family in its own home, where the dignity and identity of each individual can be respected and protected

- reassuring parents that difficulties in bringing up children are not unusual, and emphasising the pleasures of family life

- developing a relationship with a family in which time can be shared and understanding can be developed, with a flexible approach to take account of different needs

- encouraging the parents' strength and well-being for the ultimate benefit of their own children

- encouraging a family to widen its network of relationships and to use other support and services effectively within the community.

This information is taken from the Home-Start Constitution (personal communication).

Appendix 2

Outcome measures

Details of the measures

As background information for the results provided in Chapters 4 and 5, what follows is a brief overview of each of the measures and related scoring details.

The Parenting Stress Index/Short Form

The PSI/SF is a direct derivative of the Parenting Stress Index full-length test. It was developed to meet the needs of clinicians and researchers for a valid measure of stress in the parent–child system that could be completed in a short time period. It generates a Total Stress score and three subscale scores [Parental Distress (PD), Parent–Child Dysfunctional Interaction (P-CDI) and Difficult Child (DC)]. It also generates a Defensive Responding Scale (Abidin, 1995). For the purposes of this report, only the Total Stress score is reported.

Total Stress score

The Total Stress score is designed to provide an indication of the overall level of parenting stress an individual is experiencing. It does not include stresses associated with other life roles and life events. Parents who obtain a Total Stress score above a raw score of 90 (at or above the 90th percentile) are considered to be experiencing clinically significant levels of stress. Raw scores at or above 86 are considered to be experiencing a high level of stress. The normal range for scores is 56–85. Scores of 55 and less are regarded as low.

The Edinburgh Postnatal Depression Scale

The EPDS was designed by Cox *et al.* (1987) to assist primary healthcare professionals detect mothers suffering from postnatal depression. Earlier research suggests that mothers who scored above a threshold of 13 were likely to be suffering from a depressive illness of varying severity.

The Centre for Epidemiological Studies Depression Scale

The CES-D (Radloff, 1977) is a 20-item, self-report scale for use in general population studies to measure the presence and severity of depressive symptomatology. Scores above 16 are considered high.

The Rosenberg Self-Esteem Scale

The concept of self-esteem is part of the wider construct of self-concept. It is typically seen as a personal resource, which may moderate the effects of threatening events or conditions. The RSE (Rosenberg, 1965, 1989) is one of the most widely used measures. Low scores indicate high self-esteem but no cut-off point is indicated.

The Brief Infant–Toddler Social and Emotional Assessment Scale

The BITSEA was developed for the early identification of young children who may have social–emotional or behavioural problems or delays in competence (Briggs-Gowan and Carter, 2001). It was derived from the Infant–Toddler Social and Emotional Assessment Scale (ITSEA) (Carter and Briggs-Gowan, 2000) and was designed for use with 1- and 2-year-old children, but 3-year-old children can be included (M.J. Briggs-Gowan and A.S. Carter, personal communication).

This measure generates Problem and Competence scores. Problem scores that fall at or above the cut-off points are considered to represent a high level of problems. Competence scores that fall at or below the cut-off points are considered to indicate low competence. Details regarding cut-off points relevant to a child's age at first-stage analysis are provided below (Table A2.1). Combining a child's status with the Problem and Competence scores provides the most sensitive detection of problems and delays in competence. If a child has a high problem score and/or a low competence scores she or he would be considered to screen positive on the BITSEA. Where this occurs, the child would be regarded as having social–emotional or behavioural problems or delays in competence.

In this Study mothers were asked to complete the measure in respect of the same child considered for the PSI/SF where the child's age fell within the appropriate age range for this test (i.e. up to their third birthday at first interview stage). Hence the number of children (53) included in this sample was small. Only 49 mothers completed the measure at both time points.

The Maternal Social Support Index

The MSSI was developed by Pascoe *et al.* (1988) to assess the emotional and tangible support provided by a mother's social network. It provides information about the mother's perceptions of help with daily tasks (e.g. making meals), her satisfaction with relationships (e.g. with husband/partner), the availability of help in time of need (e.g. people who could care for children for a few hours) and her involvement in the community (e.g. social groups and school). Group medians are usually calculated. Scores below 15 would describe a very difficult, isolated life (J. M. Pascoe, personal communication).

Table A2.1 BITSEA score cut-off points by gender and age

	Cut-off points	
Scale	Girl	Boy
Problem		
12–17 months	13	15
18–23 months	15	15
24–29 months	13	14
30–35 months	14	14
Competence		
12–17 months	11	11
18–23 months	15	13
24–29 months	15	14
30–35 months	15	14